# CUSTOMER-CENTRIC COST REDUCTION

By Maurice FitzGerald B.E.
With Peter FitzGerald D.Phil.

i

# Copyright

Published in Switzerland
First edition, 2017

ISBN 978-2-9701172-5-4

Maurice FitzGerald Consulting
Chemin des Crêts-de-Champel
1206 Geneva
Switzerland
www.customerstrategy.net

# About the authors

Maurice FitzGerald

Maurice retired from Hewlett Packard Enterprise where he was Vice-President of Customer Experience for Software up to early 2016. Before moving to HP Software in 2012, Maurice spent six years as a member of both the overall HP EMEA Leadership Team and the EMEA Enterprise Business Management Team. He implemented HP strategies that cross all businesses and functions, with a special focus improving Enterprise customer experience with HP. Other work included business strategy development for emerging markets, vertical industries, and a variety of transformational initiatives particularly in sales. He led the EDS / HP integration work for the Enterprise Business in Europe the Middle East and Africa. He has also worked for Compaq, Digital Equipment Corporation, and Blue Bell Apparel, the parent company of Wrangler jeans at the time.

Peter FitzGerald

After his Bachelor's degree in Psychology from the National University of Ireland, Peter went on to do his doctorate in Cognitive Psychology at Oxford University. Among the important things he learned was that he needed to paint with his left hand, rather than his right. He combined early work at the Max Planck Institute in Munich with the development of a successful career as an artist. He ultimately left psychology to work in the visual arts full-time, including thirteen years as the editor-in-chief of Ireland's leading art magazine, *Circa*. In addition to artwork, Peter also designs and implements websites and newsletters for galleries and other businesses. His website is at iCulture.website.

# Acknowledgments

The last nine months spent writing this book and its two companion titles have been a fantastic learning experience. I learned how to transfer knowledge from my brain to my writing software. I also learned that the subjects I chose to write about interest a lot of people. There are several people whom I must thank for their help and guidance.

First, of course, is my brother who did all the line drawings in all three books. His artistic ability and wry sense of humor come across well. Peter's years of professional experience as the editor of Ireland's leading art magazine, CIRCA, have also been invaluable. His eagle eye caught many mistakes I would never have seen, no matter how often I read the books out loud to myself.

Our test readers provided hundreds of improvement suggestions. I particularly want to thank Alyona Medelyan, Lindsay Hall, my sisters Una and Claire, Lena Forssell, Luc Vanden Plas, Matti Airas, François Gschwindemann, Michelle Tom, and David Jacques. Dale Halvorson, Dr. James Borderick and Ian Maddrell also provided much-needed encouragement and indeed stimulation to start writing in the first place.

And I can't forget my daughter Claire's great work on the cover illustrations. She, her sister Michelle and my wife Danielle have provided the support I need on the journey so far.

# Contents

# Foreword

I was looking out my office window near Charles de Gaulle airport in 1982. The phone rang just as I was watching Concorde take off on its daily flight to New York. In hindsight, the contrast was complete. The roar of the afterburners was the symbol of no-expense-spared extravagance. The phone call was the start of the opposite: my first participation in a major corporate cost-cutting exercise.

I was no stranger to cost reduction. I graduated as an Industrial Engineer in Ireland in 1977. There was amazing demand at the time, and my entire class had signed employment contracts before our final exams. High-tech did not exist in its current form. Following a student project and summer work at Imperial Chemical Industries, I had an ICI mentor; R. T. O'Kelly, an Englishman known universally simply as RTK. He advised me not to start my career at ICI, but to choose a company that was growing quickly and would let me work in other countries. Remember this was before high-tech. I signed my contract with Blue Bell Apparel, the parent company of Wrangler Jeans, among other brands. A week after starting, I found myself in rural Commerce, Georgia with a stopwatch in my hand. Industrial Engineers were measured on saving at least 15 times their pay. I got good at it while I lived and worked in the USA, Ireland, France, Italy, Spain and Scotland, all in the space of seven years. I became an expert in warehouse automation, which turned out to pay very well in high-tech, but that is another story.

The Parisian phone call was from my boss, asking me to attend an introduction to McKinsey's Overhead Value Analysis of our company, for which I was to be a project lead. The work was my first and purest customer-centric cost reduction exercise. Keeping customers at the center of your cost-reduction work is challenging, at best. Employees who are worried about being able to feed their families don't care much about customers.

Communication of customer-centric cost reduction is also challenging. A coherent customer-centric message about priorities will be something like this: "Since we must preserve or increase spending in departments A, B and C to ensure great service to our customers, we will need to cut even more in departments X, Y and Z, which have no direct customer impact." This is a much harder message to deliver to internal team leaders than "In the spirit of fairness, everyone's budget will be cut 20%."

What follows covers different methods of cost reduction and how to maintain or improve customer loyalty as you design and implement the reductions. It is not easy. I have managed programs that made things much worse for customers too. I did not do it deliberately. I just had nobody around me with relevant experience and advice. After many years of work in the area, I now want to share some advice and experience with you.

# 1.   Introduction

# 1.1 Introduction

This book is about customer-centric cost reduction, an apparent oxymoron. Faced with a profitability crisis or a need to find money to invest, most companies want to sort out their P&L first, and worry about keeping their customers later. That approach tends to produce a corporate death-spiral. While you may be sacrificing customer happiness in the short term, your competitors may not. They will make it their business to find out where you are cutting costs and how that affects your customers. They will then go in and empathize, taking share from you. You then wind up with a predictable but unanticipated revenue problem, just as your cost-cutting exercise finishes. So, the next round of cost reduction starts. And so on.

There are only 3.5 ways of reducing costs. I will cover various methods of getting there, adding advice on how to avoid losing customers as you go about it.

## Good and bad cost reduction

Unless you are in survival mode, where almost any cost reduction is good, a good cost reduction is one that either improves things for your customers, or simply one that they will never notice. Improving things can be as simple as being able to pass on lower costs as lower prices. Process simplification can also lower costs and improve service levels.

Reductions that customers don't notice concern areas with which they have no direct contact, for example your real estate costs, or the costs of regularly changing employees' PCs.

Bad cost reduction makes things worse for customers, whether by making a product or service worse, or putting them in regular contact with demoralized employees.

# Introduction

Ways to reduce costs

While this may seem surprising, there are exactly 3.5 ways of reducing costs. The first three are:

- Fewer people
- Lower costs of capital, such as real estate and inventory
- Pay your suppliers less

More about the 0.5 below.

And two common ways cost-reduction initiatives fail

Many companies work out that they need to cut back in some areas to be able to invest in others. The two most common reasons for failure are:

# Introduction

1. Inability to effectively communicate the purpose, scope and timing of the reductions to customers, investors and employees causes delay, customer defection and employee disengagement, durably damaging your business.
2. Incompetent or inexperienced program managers define terms of reference, tasks, deliverables and milestones without involving the people who will have to do the work. All too often, this is driven by a misguided desire for total secrecy before the reductions are announced. If the people who will have to do the work do not also do the planning, there is absolutely no chance whatsoever that the reduction work will be completed as planned.

## Seems too simple?

This may seem too simple, but it is not. I have been taught many ways of making things more efficient and put most of them into practice. My bachelor's degree is in Industrial Engineering, which is all about productivity and effectiveness. Over the years, I have improved hundreds, perhaps thousands of work processes. I started in the clothing industry which is absolutely obsessed with cost. I moved on to logistics and repair centers at Digital Equipment Corporation, before migrating to software, services, alliances and hardware at DEC, Compaq and HP.

When Mark Hurd was CEO of HP, he was fanatical about cost reduction. Quite a few (thankfully, not all) of the cost improvements we implemented over the years turned out not to make any real difference to our financial results. Here is why some projects failed: the people were still there, so the people costs did not change; all buildings were still there, so those costs did not change either; we continued to pay our suppliers the same amount, so those costs remained the same.

If you improve a work process, and do not change the number of people you have in a given location, the people costs do not change. They just spend part of their time doing nothing, or find unimportant new work to do. If you reduce the amount of space you need, but keep all the buildings, your real estate costs do not change. If you make fewer demands on your suppliers, but continue to pay them the same amount, those costs don't change either.

# Introduction

## 'Making it real'

I call the process of ensuring savings ideas turn into reality 'Making it real'. In this process, anyone with a reduction project should be able to describe which line of the P&L will be impacted, and exactly how. If less work is needed, what are the names of the people who will be let go, so the Cost of Sales or SG&A lines go down? If less space is needed, who will buy or rent the free space, or which buildings will we vacate? If the savings ideas just produce fractional differences spread across the entire population or all buildings, they are not worth pursuing.

If you want to be pedantic, the first three items could be more accurately described as less people cost, less capital cost and paying suppliers less. If you move work offshore, you may reduce the cost, providing you let the onshore people go. If you move from an expensive city-center location to cheaper choices on the outskirts, you will reduce your real estate costs if you close the original building.

## And the 0.5?

The remaining half a way of reducing cost is by making one-time accounting changes. You can change the accounting treatment of certain items. You can move your HQ to a low-tax jurisdiction. You can sell your buildings and lease them back. Since your competitors can do the same, it is debatable whether they produce sustainable competitive advantage.

## I object

The objections I have heard to the above are mainly around the definitions. For example, if you make a process more efficient in a growing company, you may avoid hiring new people. That is true, but you have not actually reduced your absolute costs, which is the subject here.

## Cost reduction versus cost avoidance

Cost avoidance may feel good, but it is usually not a real thing. We will cover one aspect of cost avoidance, more correctly cost reduction avoidance after handling the main topics. I learned about it quite late in my career, as it is not intuitive. Cost reduction normally covers things that are mentioned in standard P&L, Balance Sheet and Cash Flow statements. There is one major opportunity to improve bottom-line profit that does not appear in any standard accounting statements. More on this later.

## Behavioral economics principles

Dan Ariely and Nobel-winner Daniel Kahneman are two leaders in the emerging field of behavioral economics. Their research, and that of others in the field, show convincingly that humans do not behave as traditional economists would have us believe. As Ariely puts it, we are "predictably irrational". Traditional economists would have us believe that people's reactions to reductions will be equal and opposite to their reactions to gains. This is simply not the case, and we will cover the consequences in some detail. Humans' aversion to losing something they already have is a major reason some cost reduction initiatives fail. Planning for it is essential.

## We are talking about people

Reducing costs means taking away people's space, reducing their benefits and perceived well-being, bringing fear to the workplace and sometimes ruining lives and breaking up families. As people managing cost reduction, our natural tendency is to avoid dealing with it. Change management is an essential skill and some suggestions on how to do it will be provided.

## Customer-centric cost reduction

Even employees who are not at risk of job loss will be upset if they believe the changes put customers at risk. It must be said that making large-scale reductions damages your brand and will make some customers believe you are not a safe supplier. Your competitors will be busy helping grow that perception. "We are talking about a multi-year contract here. Look at what Acme has just announced. Are you sure they will still be around two years from now?" If your employees also believe that the changes will have an unfavorable impact on customer perception of your products and services, that feeling will be communicated to your customers. To keep the maximum number of customers and employees on board, you need to understand how to put customers at the center of the reduction exercise, ensuring you make things better for them, or at least no worse, and that your entire team knows it. These are difficult messages to communicate, and even more difficult to put into practice. That is why this book exists.

# 2.  Deciding why and what to cut

## 2.1   Why cut costs?

"On the whole I'd say they took it well."

There are two main reasons companies need to cut costs:

1. Company leadership wants to invest to improve market share, and does not want to borrow more money to make those investments.
2. Company owners feel they are not getting a good enough return on their investment and want a quick improvement in profitability.

Cost-cutting to invest

This is what I would call healthy cost-cutting. The essence of business strategy is concentration of your scarce resources on things that will let you win. You win by being different from or better than your competitors. Things that make you different or better are the 'core competencies' you want to invest in and develop. There should be a limited number of them at any given time. Everything other than the core competencies should be done as efficiently as possible, meaning at the lowest cost that provides a level of quality that is acceptable to customers. Why would you try to do them better than that, as they will not make you different or better? Cost-cutting for investment purposes is difficult, but easier than for pure profit improvement. The reason is that you can communicate the investments to your employees, customers and investors in a positive way, projecting a happy future.

Cost-cutting to improve profit
If you have encountered a market disruption or have not been fortunate enough to invest at the right time, you can find yourself in different versions of survival mode. You must improve profits or stop losing money to be able to keep your investors. This sort of cost-cutting is much harder to carry out, as the only message you can honestly give to your different stakeholders is about avoiding a horribly negative future. Some of them are likely to leave you. Even if you believe you are in this situation, I would urge you to identify the investments you would like to make, if you could find the money. Let's hope the suggestions that follow will let you take that path.

Three categories of cost reduction
No matter which need drives your cost-reduction efforts, there are three categories:

1. The things that give you a competitive advantage and should be subjected to little or no cost-reduction.
2. The things that depend on knowledge that is inside your company and that would be difficult to outsource. These have to be done as efficiently as possible. If you design, manufacture, sell and support a product, the relationship between your R&D and support people may be critical to ongoing design improvements and new products. That relationship may be difficult or impossible to establish with a

third-party support provider. A middle-ground solution may be to set up your own support operation as a separate company.

3. Generic work that provides no conceivable competitive advantage. An example might be doing the payroll for your own employees. Unless you are doing it at a lower cost than a third-party payroll provider, there is no real reason to keep it inside your company.

## Scope is important

If you have been tasked with developing cost reduction ideas, getting your leadership team to agree the scope is a critical early step. Some provocation may be necessary. A woman in my Industrial Engineering class was asked to determine the main cost reduction opportunities in the largest local bread producer, Lydon's bakery. Their facility was quite automated for the time. Dolores just could not get agreement on the scope of the work.

After trying for two weeks, she decided to provoke them by submitting her simple supposedly final report. "Save 100% of all costs by shutting down the production facility and the retail operations." They were angry for about ten minutes, but Dolores was charming. The result was the correct discussion about the gross margin and operating profit objectives they had for their growing business, as well as the areas the leadership team considered to be out of scope. I believe they appreciated the provocation. The resulting efficiency project was a great success.

## 2.2 A legendary Mark Hurd speech to employees in Israel

Mark Hurd made many speeches about cost. His general philosophy was best illustrated by my favorite event, an all-employee meeting he hosted when visiting Israel.

EDS

At the time, the HP acquisition of Ross Perot's Electronic Data Systems was new news. Mark described his first meeting with the full EDS leadership team in Plano, Texas. His story went something like this:

"... and I said 'You have $25 billion in revenue and $1 billion in operating profit. I bet I can tell you what your costs are.' They seemed puzzled. They looked at each other around the table. There was an uncomfortable silence. I said 'Hey, it's not difficult. Your costs are $24 billion.' More silence. Then the CFO said, 'That can't be right.' So I asked him for the correct number. He said he would have to get back to me. Later the same day he told me the cost number was $32 billion. Interesting. Apparently 25 minus 1 equals 32 at EDS."

For the sake of fairness, I suppose I should explain that the $32 billion number was the result of a strange EDS business practice of marking up internal cost transfers. For example, if it cost the real estate people $6,000 per employee to provide office space each year, they would charge each department about $8,000, so the real estate people could fund their own investments. When reporting the cost numbers to Mark, the CFO added up all the charge-outs, rather than the true costs.

What's the point?

The point of the speech is of course that everything other than operating profit is indeed a cost. Everything, without exception. I was about 30 years

# A legendary Mark Hurd speech to employees in Israel

into my professional career and had never thought about cost that way. Of course, Mark was correct. He thought in terms of good costs and bad costs. Good costs directly drive revenue growth. Bad costs are everything else. Whether at NCR, HP or Oracle, Mark has been obsessed with ensuring there is enough cash available for good costs, particularly sales people. Anything that does not drive growth directly, including indirect things like Marketing, have always been in his reduction cross-hairs.

"With the launch of today's mission we will be one step closer to proving EDS's greatest theorem, '25 minus 1 equals 32'."

# 2.3 How to develop a cost reduction strategy

Like all types of business strategy, a cost-reduction strategy is about winning. It is about deciding what you will and will not do to give yourself a competitive advantage. Deciding what you will not do is at least as important as what you will do. Ideally, cost reduction would be an integral part of your overall business strategy. If you need to develop the cost reduction strategy on its own, there are six dimensions you should consider. There are just six. If you ask and answer appropriate questions in each, you can be certain that your approach is comprehensive.

None of what follows changes the cost-reduction objective. It simply helps you decide how to achieve it without negatively impacting your customers or your competitive position. In most companies, you will already have the data required to do the analysis described below, and should be able to complete the work within a couple of weeks. If you discover that you have no information at all in one of the dimensions, it is worth taking the time to do the work properly. This chapter provides a summary of the strategy development steps. More detail is provided for some areas in the chapters that follow.

Strategy Fails

Rookie fail                                    Still no

# How to develop a cost reduction strategy

## Customers

Studying the customer dimension answers questions in two areas. First, what are the critical things that customers admire the most about your company and that give you a competitive advantage? Second, what are the things that customers don't really notice?

If you are a normally functioning modern company, you know what it is that customers like about your products and services, and what they want you to improve. The top five items on each of these two lists should only be addressed for cost-cutting if doing so has no conceivable effect on your ability to execute them.

Prepare a simple customer journey map and identify touchpoints that cost a lot and that customers never mention in either a good or bad way. Even where customers do value or require improvement for a touch point, consider whether the high-cost ones can be done more efficiently. Please don't rely on anecdotes and opinions of your own team about what customers believe to be important. If you don't have the information and do have a list of phone numbers or email addresses, ask the customers directly. It is easy to get a three-question survey done with thousands of customers within ten days. The questions you should ask are:

- How likely are you to recommend [product, service, or company, depending on what you need to find out] to a colleague or friend? Measure this on a scale from zero to 10.
- Why?
- What would you like us to improve?

You can easily find standard templates in multiple languages for these so-called Net Promoter System®[1] surveys on surveymonkey.com and other platforms. If the nature of your business is such that a very small number of your customers make up the majority of the revenue, talk to all of them

---

[1] Net Promoter, Net Promoter System, Net Promoter Score, NPS and the NPS-related emoticons are registered trademarks of Bain & Company, Inc., Fred Reichheld and Satmetrix Systems, Inc.

individually, ideally face-to-face. Once you have this information, a good analysis technique is customer journey cost mapping, covered a couple of chapters from now.

## What customers want can surprise you, in a good way

Way back in 1999, we decided we needed to save $40 million in hardware service delivery in Europe in Compaq. We decided that we would test asking customers to do simple parts replacement themselves on desktop PCs and low-end Intel servers. We determined that it would save us about $70 per service event, compared to paying a partner or our own people to go on site. The scope was service contracts or warranties that entitled the customer to have a service engineer go on site to do the replacement. We implemented in some countries, collecting customer satisfaction data at the same time.

The surprise was the customer satisfaction was higher when the customers replaced the parts themselves. Our research suggested that this was due to two factors. First, this meant they controlled the timing. Second, they simply liked being given the choice. Happier customers and lower costs. What could be better?

## Resellers and implementation partners

If your products are sold or implemented by other companies, you need their views too. Once again, don't rely on anecdotes, and survey them if needed. You may want to consider your partners as potential sources of cost reduction, if you can transfer some types of work to them. If, for example, you have resellers who provide customers with on-site technical support or repair services for your products, perhaps they should do more of it. Resellers are often physically closer to customers and their travel costs can be much lower than those you may have when you use your own people.

Resellers and implementation partners usually want as exclusive a relationship as possible with their customers, and may therefore be happy to take over any work you currently do directly. As with customers, look at partner touchpoints with your company that require significant resources to operate and which the partners never mention when surveyed. They should be the main focus of reduction efforts.

# How to develop a cost reduction strategy

Competition

What do you believe differentiates you from your competitors? What makes you different or better? Ideally, you will only ask these questions after you have the answers to the questions about customers and partners. Since you will mainly depend on answers from your own (biased) team, only their views that agree with what customers and partners say should be considered as 100% validated. You will need to do some speculating about where your competitors will go in the future, with no obvious legal way of cross-checking it. Try to distinguish between your traditional competitors and new emerging companies. Of course, if low price is your main or only differentiator, you face a future of continuous cost-cutting.

**Exhibit 2-1**

Six situation analysis dimensions lead to powerful insights

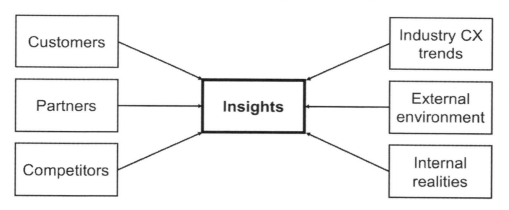

Industry dynamics

What is happening in your industry? Has there been extreme price pressure for the last five years that is expected to continue? Is modern technology changing it in a way that is making it more or less attractive to you and to your competitors? Will these changes require more or less cost reduction?

The trends are the most important factor. If the trends suggest that your costs need to go down 5% per year indefinitely, you will not be able to live with a simple one-time cost reduction exercise. Since your competitors will be subject to the same dynamics, the question to be answered is how you can do a better job of continuous cost-reduction than they can.

External factors

Are government regulations changing in a way that affects your business and your costs? How has your home-country currency been trending against those of countries where you are present over the last five or ten years? What would happen to your need to reduce costs if those trends continue? Note in passing that it is well established that nobody is any good at predicting currency trends or gold prices. You will be able to find people who have been lucky in some random estimates, but nobody who is consistently good at it over time.

For cost reduction, the most significant external factors are often the labor regulations in each country where your company is present. It can be difficult, even impossible to implement involuntary layoffs when the overall parent company is profitable. This, and working with workers' councils in Europe, need to be built into your plans. I have included a chapter on workers' councils later in this book.

All sorts of other external factors can matter. If you have a business that is dependent on the weather, you should look at climate trends, for example.

Your own ability to execute

Finally, your cost-cutting choices must consider your own ability to execute against any such plan. From a people-reduction perspective, the most important question is whether natural attrition and possible transfers in affected areas mean that you won't have to organize layoffs. Where layoffs are needed, we will consider some of the execution challenges later in this book, like how to take unions and workers' councils into account.

If you have never undertaken a similar cost-cutting exercise before, you should not trust your own timing estimates. Ask others who have done similar things, then adjust that timing based on what you feel will be harder or easier in your situation. If you only see things that will be easier for you, you are probably not looking hard enough. Execution is also about communication. Loss-aversion is a major part of human psychology, and the path to major reductions will not be easy, whether it be for customers, employees or other stakeholders.

## Timing of the situation analysis

The six dimensions above constitute your Situation Analysis. If you already have the data, or are a small company, it should take no more than two weeks to prepare. For a large company or if you lack some of the data, it may take four to six weeks.

## Develop insights and make your choices

Once you have examined each of these areas, you will know whether cost-reduction is something you need to do one time, or whether it has to be a permanent way of life. You should have identified a 'long list' of reduction opportunities. If you have sized the opportunities, they should add up to two to three times the reductions you actually need, as not every reduction idea will be realistic. You now need to go from the long list to a shorter list of proposals for your leadership team. It is critical that those decisions be made with the involvement of those who will drive the implementation.

## Conclusion

There are no other major factors that matter in your decision-making process. The secret to getting new answers in each area is to ask new questions. Most should be questions that will use unbiased data sources as references for your answers. Bias will be prevalent within your company as each leader will want to minimize the amount of unattractive reduction work they must do personally.

# 2.4  Cost reduction and hygiene factors

Various theories about motivation include the concept of 'hygiene factors'. These are things like taking a shower, where doing more than a certain amount brings no additional benefit. Some hygiene factors are as basic as air. If you can breathe, you don't notice it. Giving you more air than you need to breath normally adds no value.

## Hygiene factors and delighting customers

A common customer experience slogan is "We must delight customers at every possible interaction." While it sounds nice, it is nonsensical. Not many interactions matter. Basic service center interactions are a good example. If you have resolved the customer's issue, that is good enough. Doing more does not add anything and wastes money.

## Hygiene factors and customer-centric cost reduction

The heart of customer-centric cost reduction is understanding which of your activities just have to be 'good enough'. Once they are good enough, they are not worthy of further investment. If such 'above and beyond' investments have already been made, they should be cut back. They serve no purpose. There is a challenge, and that is how to determine whether the work areas in question are indeed good enough. Here are some indicators:

1. Common sense applies. You probably have costs that are totally invisible to customers, and which have no conceivable impact on them. For example, your customers really don't care how much you pay for office supplies. They probably don't care about the cost of some building they never visit. Assuming the basics function, they don't care about your telecommunications costs. These sorts of costs can be reduced without affecting customer loyalty and growth.

2. Use your existing customer survey data to find out what customers care about. If you have a complaints department, you have a good source of information about things that may not be good enough,

even if they should be hygiene factors. If you believe your service center hold times are fine, but your customers are irritated by them and say your competitors do a better job, then you should probably not cut costs in a way that makes the hold times worse. Note that it would also be a waste of energy to identify and communicate fifty hygiene factors. I suggest keeping your list to three to five things that are easy for everyone to remember.

3.  While customer surveys are a great source for data on what customers care about and how you compare to competitors, not all survey types are useful for this purpose. The useful ones include open questions that ask customers what they would like to see improved, or for their reasons for giving an overall satisfaction rating of some type. If you do not have this type of question in your research, you risk cutting expenses where it is not appropriate. Many survey types require customers to choose between a set of options that you have dreamed up, but which may not reflect their reality. Think about this as the only question a waiter might ask in a restaurant: "Would you like your steak rare, medium-rare, medium or well-done?" But you do not get the choice of having something other than steak or being a vegetarian. If you are the restaurant owner, ask the open question "What would you like to eat today?" If nobody ever asks for a vegetarian option, you can safely remove it from your menu.

4.  More common sense applies, in the absence of survey data. It should be obvious that a number of transactional processes just have to work. If you accept credit cards, the credit card approval/denial process must be almost instantaneous. No normal customer could be 'delighted' by their credit card being approved, and nobody would recommend your company based only on the approval. Similarly, if your service center solves a customer issue, most customers will consider that to be acceptable, but could not be 'delighted' about it. After all, they did not expect or want to have an issue to resolve in the first place. Once you believe your issue resolution is as good as that of your competitors, you should do it as inexpensively as possible. The same applies to processes associated with renewing existing service contracts, for example.

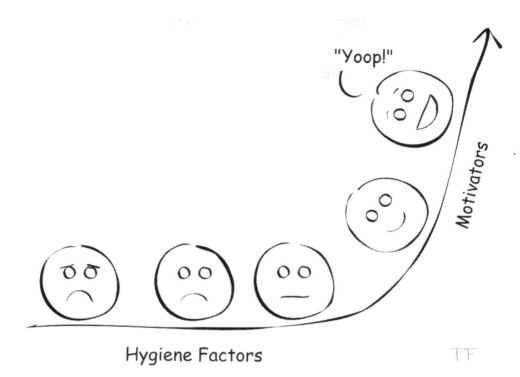

## Implications for cost-reduction goals

For the sake of simplicity, let's suppose half your people costs are for work on hygiene factors, and half on things that genuinely make customers happy, generate recommendations and drive loyalty. Customer-centric cost-reduction means that your savings should come entirely from the hygiene factor work, with one major condition. That work has to already be 'good enough'. In the absence of a precise definition of good enough, it needs to be as good as your main competitors.

## Implications for your organization

If you do indeed respect these guidelines, it will become clear to your employees that there are areas that are good for career development and others that will be relatively depressing places to work, under constant cost pressure. Your hygiene factors will not be the same as those of companies specialized in that type of work. You should consider achieving the cost-savings by using Business Process Outsourcing (BPO) services. Your hygiene factors are their core business. Your people may be happier being transferred to the outsourcing company.

## Negotiating a good BPO contract

Business Process Outsourcing contracts tend to be long-term in nature. Five- to seven-year terms are common, and I have even seen a twenty-year contract agreement with a Swiss bank. A typical contract is for a 20% cost-reduction, usually measured in cost per transaction. For example, if you outsource the processing of expense claims, the contract will be for a 20% cost reduction per claim within a defined period of time. Standard contracts include renegotiation clauses. Save yourself the hassle by negotiating further ongoing price reductions, for example 1% per year, directly into the contract when you sign it.

## 2.5  Danger - Benchmarking

Deloitte and other consulting companies sell benchmarking services. It is also possible to consult your competitors' annual reports and construct your own high-level benchmark comparisons. Benchmark data should be considered as interesting, but probably useless. I realize this is not what the major consulting companies on the planet believe and want to sell. Let's discuss.

Benchmarking supposes comparisons are fair

A perfectly fair cost comparison with another company would require it to be pursuing the same business strategy as you are. Exactly the same. I have never heard of a case where two competing companies described themselves as having exactly the same strategies. Understanding where your strategies are different takes time. Meanwhile, your CEO is waiting for your plan to implement the same cost structure as Deloitte (or whoever) has proposed. The proposals are normally composites, taking the lowest sales cost, the lowest marketing costs, the lowest Days Sales Outstanding and so on, across multiple competitors, each of whom has a different strategy.

Benchmarking supposes you do the same tasks as your competitors

One of the first benchmarking comparisons I ever saw compared high-tech companies by revenue per employee. Since no rationale was provided for a higher number being better or worse, the readers' intuitions naturally jumped to the incorrect conclusion that more revenue per employee was always better. When I first saw such comparisons with other companies for Digital and Compaq, we were manufacturing almost everything internally, with our own employees. We were being compared to companies, such as Apple, who subcontracted almost everything. If these companies did so rationally, they decided that they could not manufacture at the same costs as the subcontractors. Alternatively, their view might have been that even though they could do it as cheaply, they did not want to spend management attention on manufacturing, and accepted that they were transferring profit to the subcontractors. DEC and Compaq manufactured extremely cost-effectively. I feel we got tired of being harassed by journalists and analysts about irrelevant benchmark data and chose to subcontract many things we should have kept in-house. Irrational intuitive reactions to benchmark data won out.

## An example: Compaq and Tandem

Tandem produced highly fault-tolerant computers for use in financial services. At one point, all major stock exchanges in the world used the Tandem Non-Stop architecture, and many still do. Compaq bought Tandem for $3 Billion in 2007, a year before the HP-Compaq merger was announced. Tandem had a direct selling model. Compaq sold exclusively through resellers in most countries.

Joe McNally (who was employee number one in Compaq UK, and died in 2012) did his own sales benchmarking. Tandem had 27 sales people in the UK. He is alleged to have told the Tandem UK manager (Mike Hender) that he should only need a single sales person to make the same revenue. Since Joe was feeling generous, the Tandem leader was allowed to keep three.

Sales naturally collapsed completely. Re-hiring and recovery took multiple years. A correct benchmark was possible. It would have included all of the Compaq resellers' sales people, not just the sales-coded Compaq employees. Being as fair as possible to Joe, he probably expected the Tandem leader to train the Compaq resellers. That still would not have made much difference, as Tandem products had a long and complex buying cycle.

## Benchmarking gives you great hindsight

Perhaps most seriously, benchmarking is about the past, and you are trying to have an appropriate cost structure for the future. Even if you find a company with an identical strategy and a lower cost structure, it will be of limited help. First, the data is necessarily about where the competitor has been in the past. Second, by the time you achieve the cost structure the competitor used to have, they will be doing something else, with a different cost structure.

# Danger - Benchmarking

"Call me crazy, but I say the puck was here scarcely ten seconds ago."

## Lower is not necessarily better

The following example might sound sarcastic or ironic. It is not. It is a reflection of the way many companies are managed today. Let's suppose your company is embarking on an international expansion. You have decided that the greatest growth opportunity you have in the next five years is in Indonesia. You have hired a local management team. You have hired sales people and recruited local partners. You have your first orders. The benchmarking consultants arrive at your company HQ, a long way from Indonesia. They show that the market leader in your industry has half the cost per revenue dollar that you have in Indonesia. (This is of course either because they have no plan to treat Indonesia as a major growth country, or because they have already been there for the last ten years.) Your Indonesian team is therefore ordered to fire half its people, in the name of cost-competitiveness.

While this might seem like an unrealistic extreme, it is not. I have seen benchmarking comparisons with companies that have no presence in a particular country, notably in African countries, be used as a justification to shut down operations there. All I can say is that it is certainly a way of matching the competitors' benchmark revenue (zero) in those countries. When you are a multinational, it is unrealistic to expect costs to be the same everywhere you do business. Some of your customers are multinationals too, and may select you over companies that do business in fewer countries, simply because of your presence. After all, if they are present in a country

29

where you are not, they will need to set up a relationship with an additional supplier in that country.

Advice

If you are presented with a set of benchmark comparisons, be sure to start by comparing business strategies. How are the competitors spending in areas they have announced as their growth focus areas? How are they spending in more mature areas, where they are milking revenues from older products?

Ensure that you are making comparisons that are relevant. To use a software example: don't accept a simple comparison of R&D costs to revenue. Insist on three categories: incubator products with little or no revenue, but hopefully a great future; mainstream products that have been introduced two or more years ago, and where you see an ongoing need to add functionality; mature products where you are only addressing bug fixes and updates to ensure compatibility with operating system updates, for example. Each should have very different R&D-to-revenue ratios. These are somewhat similar to the Boston Consulting Group Matrix categories mentioned earlier.

Once you have compared business strategies, ensure you are looking towards the future. If a competitive benchmark cost in a particular area, for example advertising, is lower than yours, but has been increasing by 30% a year for the last five years, you should be looking at where the competitor is going, not where they have been in the past.

## 2.6   BCG Matrix

Bruce Henderson created the Boston Consulting Group 'Growth-Share Matrix' in 1970. It is used to help companies to analyze their investments. It remains an excellent tool that assists in determining where cost reduction is appropriate, and where it might be counterproductive.

**Exhibit 2.2**

Boston Consulting Group Matrix

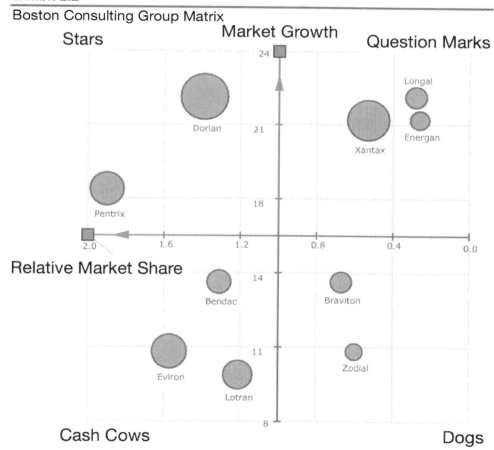

# Deciding why and what to cut

## The matrix
Each product or product family is categorized depending on relative market growth and market share. The underlying assumption is that the total amount of investment funding available is fixed. The exercise is to determine how best to split the available funds. The example below is interesting in that all of the company's products are in growing markets. If the same product, together with its share and growth numbers, were positioned in a different company's BCG matrix, it might well be in a different quadrant. The comparisons are relative, not absolute. The image in Exhibit 2.2 is from Wikipedia[2].

## An obvious dimension is missing
The time dimension is missing from the chart. A product you have just launched, or indeed one that is in development but not yet launched, will be on the right side of the chart. The setup of the matrix means you are encouraged to react more negatively to things on the right. Indeed, I feel that if a cognitive psychologist were to design the BCG matrix, high market share would be on the right, rather than the left. Our intuition is that things in the top-right are the best, and the top-left is the 'Stars' quadrant for BCG. For the sake of further discussion, assume you have one matrix for products that have been introduced more than a year ago, and another for newer products.

## Competitive comparison
To use the BCG matrix competently, you need to use it competitively, rather than exclusively filling out the graph with your own products. The real question for the Braviton product (in the Dogs quadrant above) is how it compares to the market leader and other players in its own market. The graph shows a snapshot of the Braviton position, but tells you nothing about its trend. After all, if Braviton is in a market growing at 14%, but is itself growing at 5%, it will lose share. I suggest adding share trend arrows, which would result in a graph like Exhibit 2.3.

---

[2] BCG matrix; author Ericmelse; source Wikipedia at
https://commons.wikimedia.org/wiki/File:Folio_Plot_BCG_Matrix_Example.png

**Exhibit 2.3**

Boston Consulting Group Matrix with trend arrows

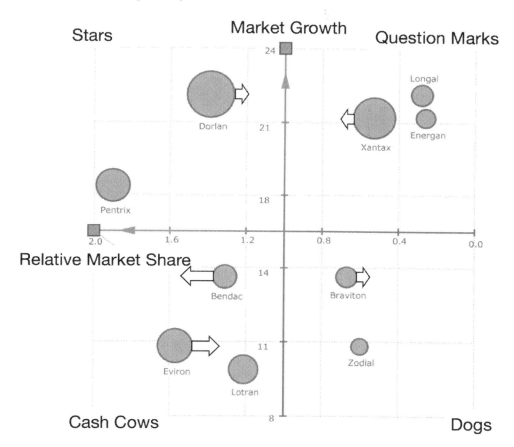

Add customer satisfaction benchmarks

If your products are covered by customer satisfaction benchmarks, add them into your decision mix. Net Promoter Score® benchmark trend comparisons with your leading competitors, for example, are excellent predictors of revenue and market share trends. This is logical. If your customers hate your products and love your competitors', you are going to lose share.

# Deciding why and what to cut

## Add profitability
Of course, growing your market share while you are losing money on each sale is not very intelligent. While the basic BCG matrix uses the bubble size to represent revenue, you should prepare a second one that uses bubble size to represent profit. The combination of all of these factors provides an initial view.

## Inter-dependencies
The BCG matrix, adjusted with growth and satisfaction trends, provides an excellent way of screening divestment candidates, or simply a way of deciding which unprofitable products to stop. However, I will always remember a business case we studied at the INSEAD. Our class was presented with a company that lost money on every single product they sold. The company also had a highly profitable services business that was growing rapidly. The way the case was presented encouraged the reader to decide to kill off the product business, or sell it to a competitor. Every single working group went this way.

We were then told that the company was actually Boeing. At the time of our course, the 737 had not yet become profitable, and indeed Boeing had never made a profit on any commercial jet they had sold. Their service business was of course entirely dependent on selling the jets. There are lots of other possible examples like razors and blades, printers and ink, and so on. The message here is that your products are not necessarily independent of each other, and the BCG matrix assumes they are. I suggest using different colors to denote the level of mutual independence.

## Conclusion
The BCG matrix is a useful analysis tool that will help you understand the relative performance of your different products. Adding the time dimension is critical to your cost-reduction decisions. While a particular product may not currently be a low-investment cash cow, that may well be where you want to position it 18 months from now, as a newer product takes over some of its market. In that case, you can start the cost reductions now.

# 2.7 Customer journey cost mapping

If you are certain your cost-reduction work will involve identifying people to let go, customer journey mapping can serve as a useful prioritization tool. There are quite a number of good ways to do journey mapping. I have found the journey map structure in Exhibit 2.4 to be particularly useful for business-to-business processes.

### Exhibit 2.4

Customer Journey Map with major customer touch points in boxes

| Product | Pricing | Lead / Opportunity | Configure Price, Quote | Order | Fulfill | Licensing/ Entitlement | Billing/ Invoicing | Rev Mgmt. & Reporting | Support Services |
|---|---|---|---|---|---|---|---|---|---|
| New Product Innovation | Organization & Governance | Opportunity Management | Select | Subscription Creation | Service Provisioning | Customer Definition | Consolidated Billing/Invoicing | Rev Rec. & VSOE | Software Updates |
| Product Development | Analytics & Price Setting | Forecast / Pipeline Mgmt. | Configure | Subscription Configuration | Access Issuance | Rights Management | Credit Management | Report Revenue | Project Mgmt./Acct |
| Product Go-to-Market | Pricing Strategy | SW Try and Buy | Price | Order Management | Cloud / Service Brokering | Access to Support & Updates | Consumption Metering | Forecast Revenue | Training |
| Ongoing Product Mgmt. | Pricing Execution | Lead Generation | Structure | Credit Management | License Key Generation | Entitlement Reporting | Manage Receivables | | Labor Tracking |
| Product Retirement | Technology & Data | Lead/Territory Management | Approve | Order Cancellation | Electronic SW Delivery | Compliance Monitoring | Collections & Disputes | | Deliver support |
| | Partner Management | | Generate Output | Renewals/ Terminations | Registration & Activation | SW Tagging / Deployment Tracking | | | |
| | Customer Engagement | | Convert | Order Integration | Cloud Service Management | | | | |
| | | | | | 3rd Party Fulfillment | | | | |

Processes in **boxes** are significant customer touchpoints

## How to prioritize

There are three factors that should each be rated as High, Medium or Low. Since 'High' has to have the same good / bad connotation for all three, these definitions may seem a little counter-intuitive:

- Number of people: the approximate number of people who work on a touchpoint. This gives you the relative savings opportunity. If you have only a few touch points in your mix that occupy a lot of people, try to be sure that they all do the same work. You may need to subdivide.

- 'Hygiene factor' rating: the degree to which customers do or do not mention the touchpoint as a reason for recommending your company. If you use the Net Promoter System, things that are never mentioned by customers who score you between 7 and 10 get a High rating. If customers only ever mention the touchpoint to complain about it, it is a hygiene factor. If it is never mentioned at all, it is a hygiene factor with high performance. The items outlined in black above are tasks that involve direct customer interaction.
- Current performance rating: the degree to which customers suggest the touchpoint needs to be improved. If customers never mention it as needing improvement, the performance rating is High.

The combination of the three ratings is an effective way of prioritizing touchpoints for reduction efforts. If, for example, your invoicing process is highly manual, never mentioned as a reason for recommending your company or products, and never mentioned as needing improvement, it might have a rating of 'High / High / High'. This would put it towards the top of the list of items to be examined for cost improvement. 'High / High / High' items are probably those where competitive benchmark cost information can be the most useful for setting reasonable cost targets, assuming you can obtain it at that level of detail.

## Top reduction priorities are mainly but not exclusively elsewhere

By definition, any work that is not on a competent customer journey map does not directly touch the customer. In a customer-centric cost reduction scenario, that is where the reduction efforts should concentrate. There is one major exception, and that is the research and development work involved in creating your new products and services and bringing them to market. It is perhaps unfortunate, but most new product development takes place without any direct customer contact. I am not suggesting that you should not look at cost reduction opportunities in product development, simply that a different approach is needed. One possibility is covered in the next chapter.

# 2.8　Span of Control and Layers

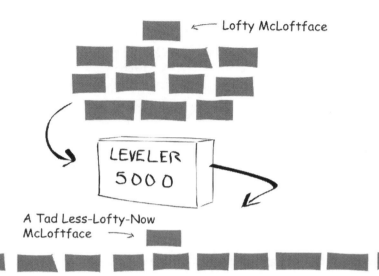

Lofty McLoftface

LEVELER 5000

A Tad Less-Lofty-Now McLoftface

Al of the major consulting companies offer consultancy on span of control and layers. They are superficially attractive, and have a number of pitfalls.

Definitions
'Span of control' (SPOC) refers to the number of employees that report directly to a given manager. Consulting companies often include it in benchmark studies. They typically advise goals of 12 to 1, meaning 12 employees reporting to one manager. The challenges in approaching SPOC correctly are the following:

- A typical SPOC analysis will identify three managers who each have four people reporting to them, and will then propose that all twelve employees should report to one of the three, and the other two managers should be fired. For this to be logical, 'managing' would have to be the full-time work of all three people managers, and they would do no individual work at all. This never ever happens. If you force this sort of combination to happen without correct analysis, important work will stop, and it may take some time before you discover the consequences.

- Under Mark Hurd's leadership at HP, temporary contract workers were not counted in the SPOC analysis. There were departments, such as service centers, where as many as 60% of the people were temps. This created post-cut situations where people managers had 20 to 30 direct reports, and were unable to make their departments function effectively. Don't be tempted to take this approach. The result is a natural manager motivation to decrease the use of temporary workers, moving to a higher number of (usually) more expensive permanent people, even if your business is highly seasonal and you don't need to have the same level of staffing all year round.

'Layers' refers to the total number of management reporting levels from the top to the bottom of your company. Having less is always good, though it not clear that it has any direct effect on cost. Top-down and bottom-up communication become less clear each time there is an additional organizational layer. Studies at HP also showed that employee happiness decreased with each layer in the organization, reaching its lowest at the bottom of a particular business structure that had 10 layers at the time.

### Useful for M&A synergies

SPOC and layer analysis are very useful when you are merging two companies that have similar businesses. There is, however, an additional rule that applies: "Don't screw up things you don't understand." If your study of the two populations shows vast differences in the numbers of people doing what seems to be the same work, it is a safe bet that the work is not the same. An example may help. When HP and EDS merged, the number of people in finance at EDS was a multiple of the number at HP. The core reason was that EDS did P&L accounting by customer for each of its major IT outsourcing contracts. HP did not. Cost pressures at the time meant the people preparing customer-specific P&Ls were eliminated. It took almost two years before we understood how much we needed them, and several more years to get reasonably good customer-specific accounting back.

When HP and Compaq merged, organizations were designed to have a specific number of direct reports per manager, on average. We also had a rule that within a country, the overall number of people managers at each job level had to reflect the 52% to 48% HP to Compaq ratios of the overall population. While this meant that many sub-optimal people choices were made, it was at least observable as fair. Nobody could say "Look, all the [insert company name] people are getting the good jobs." It was easy to show that this was not true.

# 2.9   Sometimes the best process is no process

Continuous improvement is a common catchphrase. It is easy to believe that making every existing process more efficient should be the focus. But what about eliminating the processes altogether?

### HP Lean Six Sigma training

My team was responsible for the formal regional Lean Six Sigma process improvement training at HP. Like many large companies, we designated the various training levels by using judo-like 'belt' colors. The annual Black Belt training class lasted two weeks and was always held close to Lyon, in France. Twenty to thirty 'Green Belt' process improvement experts took their skills to the following level. My job was to provide a motivational speech at the start of each session, emphasizing the importance of the work, and how it fit the corporation's overall strategy. The part about 'no process' sometimes being the best solution went something like this:

"Let's talk about a specific example of process improvement. I want to talk about a process you have all followed recently: the travel approval process you all used to get here. First, I would like to ask all those who needed four or more people to approve their travel to raise their hands." About half the class would raise their hands at this point. "I have a question for all those who raised their hands: does HP policy require you to have four levels of approval to travel here?" The unanimous answer was always in the affirmative. "OK, now, how many people needed three levels of approval to travel?" About a quarter of the class would raise their hands. "So, four-level-approval people, did the three-approval people violate a company rule?" Following a short discussion, I would ask for the people who needed two approvals and one approval. There were always some of each.

The discussion usually got quite intense at this point, but it soon became more interesting. The training host, Paul Maguire, worked for me, as well as the main trainer, John Holland. "Two people have not raised their hands yet. Paul and John, how many approvals did you need? "None." "That's right people. There is no HP policy that requires approval for travel. Your management chains have invented processes that are not actually formal requirements. I trust my team. Now… let's have a coffee break." A chaotic and loud coffee break always followed.

### Not just theory

When I joined the software leadership team, I was happy to discover that there was no formal travel approval process for the 13,000-strong organization. Trust ruled, and the senior leaders were expected to live within their overall cost budgets. Individual cost line items were strong suggestions. Mike Salfity ran the Exstream software business within the HP Imaging and Printing Group. IPG had a detailed and difficult travel approval process, one I felt was mainly designed to discourage people from even asking. Exstream was transferred to the software division. The head of software asked me to hand-hold the transfer process. Mike phoned me to find out how our travel approval process worked. Here is how it went:

> *"Maurice, I have a big spreadsheet of travel requests here. What should I do with it? Send it to you?"*
> *"No Mike. Just delete it. We trust you."*
> *"… … [Lengthy silence] … This is the happiest day of my professional career."*

OK, that example may be entertaining, but does not represent much of a cost-saving.

### Eliminating inspection

I learned about process elimination quite early in my career. During the McKinsey Overhead Value Analysis in Paris that I mentioned in the foreword, I started to question the value of inspecting completed orders. There were about 20 order pickers in the warehouse. They picked up printed order forms, took garments from shelves and put them into cartons. An automated conveyor system took them to one of three inspectors who checked that the contents did indeed match the orders. I did some random sampling and found that errors still slipped through. After following some order pickers with a stopwatch and noticing a few mistakes being made, I organized a group discussion. I asked whether the pickers noticed the errors. They said they thought they might have made mistakes, but did not check because they knew everything would be checked for them later.

I decided to run a test. First, I put a proper random sampling process in place after the final inspection, just for one week. Then I spoke to the pickers again, saying I wanted to eliminate the final inspection, and trusted them to check their orders if they felt they might have made a mistake. The results were both clear and surprising after just one week. The random sampling process found about half the number of errors, compared to the prior process following 100% inspection. Trusting people, and ensuring they know you trust them, works.

For the sake of completeness, I will mention that I then wanted to better target the random inspection process. Whenever we received a new product line, I had each size weighed and recorded in the product database. The correct weight for each order was then printed on the picking notes. Every carton had to be weighed for shipping in any case. We moved to inspecting only the cartons where the actual and theoretical weights did not match. Overall, we reduced cost and improved delivery accuracy.

## A side-note: customers did not care about delivery accuracy

I learned a lesson about this particular cost reduction when I did some customer research. It turned out that none of the store owners I surveyed cared about delivery accuracy in any case. I suppose we were good enough for it not to be a major issue. Their philosophy went like this, "If your delivery arrives on a Thursday, we will try to sell it over the weekend anyway, even if you sent us the wrong things. If we can't sell it, we will send it back the following Monday." I certainly won't go as far as to say that we should just have put random things in the cartons, but this was an area where we could safely cut costs, without taking any significant risk of losing business.

# 2.10 Example - Overall HP objectives

Quite soon after he started at HP, Mark Hurd decided we needed to find major amounts of money to invest in growth. What follows here is a description of how the objectives and metrics for our top- and second-level scorecards were set up under his leadership. No business advisory consultants were used during this exercise, as eliminating the use of such companies was one of the sub-projects. Mark and the leadership team developed it all on their own.

### Exhibit 2.5

HP top-level cost scorecard elements

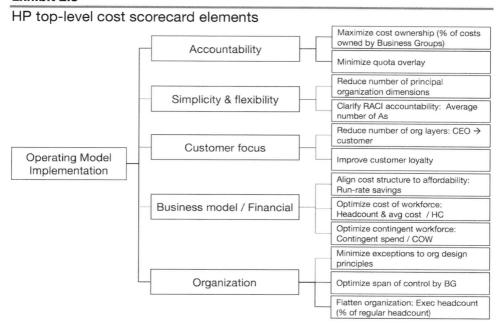

### Overall scorecard

Exhibit 2.5 shows the structure of the overall scorecard. Once it became obvious that the initiatives had had a positive impact on our financial results

43

and stock price, I was authorized to present the approach to our customers, with slightly disguised metrics. The objective of the discussions was of course to see how HP could help customers achieve the same sort of success. Details of the work and objectives for each of the five areas in the middle column of in Exhibit 2.5 follow below.

## Accountability

Mark was struck by how little control each Business Group had over its own cost structure. Central functions were authorized to make their own investments independently of any consideration of how the resulting increases in cross-charges would affect Business Group profitability. The objective of the new initiative was to increase the proportion of costs under direct control of the businesses from 50% to 70%.

This was mainly done by changing reporting lines of Marketing and Sales teams, for example. We also reduced the number of people who were compensated on the same deal. Such double- (or more) compensation structures are known as quota overlay. Before the changes, three to four people received sales-related compensation in addition to the sales person who carried legal quota and actually won the business. After the change, this varied between 1.5 and 2, depending on the Business Group.

## Simplicity & flexibility — Organization dimensions

When Mark Hurd joined HP, we had a printer group, a PC group, a Technology Solutions Group (TSG) and a Customer Solutions Group (CSG). CSG was structured by industry. TSG had sales specialists who understood individual products very well, though not the overall solutions being sold to customers.

Most of the CSG sales team were moved into the TSG organization, and the industry dimension was eliminated, leaving products and countries as the only sales structures. To make this palatable, all of the formal country managing director positions were given to the CSG leaders. Corporate functions still existed, of course. The result of the organizational dimension changes was therefore a move from four to three: PCs, Printers, and TSG.

# Example – Overall HP objectives

Simplicity & flexibility — RACI accountability

A RACI diagram describes who is Responsible for doing work, who is Accountable, meaning has the approval authority, who must be Consulted while the work is done, and who must be Informed after it is complete. An example is below. A rule is that there must be only a single 'A' on any row. Multiple Rs are OK. The problem Hurd wanted to address was that multiple people believed they were accountable for many decisions. The average was about two 'As' for each major work area, and we wanted to reduce it to as close to one as possible.

Exhibit 2.6 is an example of a RACI chart adapted from Wikipedia[3].

## Exhibit 2.6

RACI chart example

### Maintenance Crew KPI RACI Chart

| Tasks | Maint Supervisors | Maint Analyst | Maint Planner | Maint Technician | Maint Superintend | Rel Specialist | CMMS Project Engr |
|---|---|---|---|---|---|---|---|
| Inputting Failure Data | A | C | I | R | | C | C |
| Work Order Completion | R | C | C | C | A | I | I |
| Work Order Close Out | C | R | C | | I | I | A |
| QA of Failure Data input | C | R | I | C | I | C | A |
| Analyze Failure Reports | C | C | I | C | A | R | I |
| Maintenance Strategy Adjustments | C | I | I | C | A | R | R |
| Implementing New Strategies | R | I | R | C | A | I | I |

Responsibility: "The Doer"
Accountable: "The Buck Stops Here"
Consulted: "In the Loop"
Informed: "Kept in the Picture"

I remember my first somewhat-traumatic experience with an excessively complex approval process. I wanted to propose an investment in a joint go-to-market with the now-defunct Baan software company. I was very well-

---

[3] RACI chart example is 'from the maintenance and reliability community' and was taken from Wikipedia at https://en.wikipedia.org/wiki/Responsibility_assignment_matrix

prepared and had researched exactly who had the relevant decision authority, according to company policy. I dialed in to the approval teleconference, expecting to meet a chairperson, a finance person and the approver. Eight other people were on the call too. Being somewhat naïve at the time, I asked why the additional people were there, since they had no role in the approval process. In short, they all recognized that they did not have the authority to say yes, but believed they did indeed have the authority to say no. My reaction did not make me popular with eight people on the phone.

## Customer focus — layers

When I literally gave a (sadly non-functioning) magic wand to the co-CEO of Sony-Ericsson with a video camera running some years ago, I asked him to make three wishes. The wishes were for ways that HP could make his business more successful or his life easier. His third completely unprompted wish was for fewer layers between the CEO and the HP sales people he met. He felt the CEO (Léo Apotheker at the time) was too distant from the sales people and thereby too far from customers. Léo addressed this by appointing a global head of sales, Jan Zadak, as a direct report. Meg Whitman subsequently reversed the decision and did away with the separate global sales function, but that is another story.

Turning the clock back to Mark Hurd's time, when he joined HP, there were 11 organizational layers between him and the customers, at the most distant point. There were about 145,000 people in the company, so radical change was not really possible. His goal was to move to 9 layers for the largest business, which included break-fix support services, and lower numbers for other functions, for example six layers for sales. While that might still seem a lot, think about the number of countries on the planet. A sales person in Morocco necessarily reported to a manager in Morocco, who in turn reported to a manager for a group of countries, then to the Europe, Middle East and Africa leader, who in turn reported at corporate level.

## Customer focus — Customer Loyalty Index

Perhaps oddly, this was the only metric that Mark did not inspect regularly. It was a composite customer happiness metric that combined three other metrics. The relationship between the metric and actual customer loyalty was well-proven, though I suppose the time lag involved did not fit Hurd's desire to review everything at least once a month.

### Business model / Financial

The cost-saving sub-metrics to achieve the annual $3 billion savings are covered below. To an extent, it is fair to say that the $3B number was the master metric for everything else. As a subset of that we had a goal to reduce the number of employees slightly, as well as reducing the average cost per employee. As should be expected, reducing the average employee cost included some centralization and moves of work to lower-cost locations. To prevent balloon-squeezing, meaning the simple move of employee costs to some other cost category, we also had a goal of reducing the proportion of labor expense represented by temporary contractors and outsourcing.

### Business model / Financial — Cost of workforce — reducing pay

When we first saw the goals for reducing the average cost per employee, they seemed impossible to achieve. How little we knew! The main way it was done was by reducing everyone's pay by 5, 10 or 15%, depending on job level. Mark reduced his own pay by 20%.

Since mandatory pay reductions were not legal in a number of European countries, executives were expected to 'volunteer' to have their pay cut, while the general employees' pay was left untouched in those countries. 100% volunteering was the clear expectation, and it was tracked by individual. As an executive in Switzerland, where mandatory pay cuts were not legal, I did indeed 'volunteer'. One subtlety in all of this was that the annual bonuses were not held by the countries and Business Groups, but at corporate level. Our bonus system was simultaneously made more attractive, which made the pill easier to swallow.

(As an aside, when Léo Apotheker took over as CEO, one of his first moves was to reverse all of the salary reductions, though he kept the new bonus systems in place. Yay!)

# Deciding why and what to cut

Business model / Financial — Cost of workforce — average pay
A second approach to ensuring competitive labor costs was to compare our pay to that of the competition. There were two metrics used to monitor progress: Competitive Index and Compensation Ratio.

- The Competitive Index was established once a year by a respected consulting company who are specialized in the subject. The average pay in each geographical area for each job and job level was researched in great detail and compared to the HP pay scales. In principle, the mid-point of each of our pay scales was then set at the competitive average.
- Each business and country's average pay per 'job code' was then compared to the middle of the pay scale to establish the Compensation Ratio. If the compensation ratio was exactly 1.00, for example, this meant that our average pay for the position was exactly the same as the average pay in the market.

Mark Hurd set the goal for the HP Compensation Ratio at around 0.9, meaning our objective was to pay around 90% of the average, giving us a considerable cost advantage. While this might at first seem unreasonable, it was accompanied by strong graduate hiring programs and other methods of trying to get younger people into the workforce. Younger people were far more likely to be lower on the pay scales. Indeed, the high end of each pay scale tended to be occupied by people who performed quite well, and had been in the same job or at least at the same job level for many years. The principles were clear and worked quite well. The only way the system could be 'gamed' was to give unwarranted promotions to people who were high on a pay scale, ensuring they would be lower on the following one. Not much of that seemed to happen.

Organization
We had loads of exceptions to the theoretical organization design, particularly in smaller countries. Mark decided that he would allow a total of five structural exceptions, and we did indeed use them. Increasing the average number of employees who reported to a manager was a major component of the effort to lay off managers. The initial goal was to increase

the average by one employee per manager, though the objective was higher in some organizations. A huge management challenge was that Mark did not want temporary contractors to count in the calculation. The result was an unacceptably high average team size in some large service centers. The last top-level metric was a reduction in the overall proportion of executives, meaning Directors, Vice-Presidents, Senior VPs and Executive VPs. This reduction was less ambitious than the goals for the increases in numbers of direct reports per manager and the reduction in layers, so it was achieved without significant effort.

## Centralize goals, democratize decisions

One of Hurd's core tenets was that the goals should be centralized, and should not change. Detailed decisions about how to reach the goals were decentralized. We knew we could come back with alternate ways of reaching the same cost-saving goals, within reason. We also knew that it was pointless to ask for the goals to be changed.

# 3.    How to achieve reduction goals

# 3.1  Introduction, and the 'Golden Rule'

We have covered the basics of why cost reductions may be necessary and a way to decide what reductions to prioritize so that your customers will not be negatively affected. Most of the rest of this book is about how to go about implementing the reductions. A number of common themes occur consistently:

- Effective communication, with customers, partners, employees, executives, and indeed with employee representatives is critical to moving ahead quickly. The longer cost-reduction initiatives take to complete, the more they risk damaging your business.
- Lots of examples are provided from personal experience. I share success stories, as well as mistakes that I have made and that you can now avoid.
- Change-management and program-management processes should be evident throughout, and there are chapters on each.

Cost reduction decisions always have consequences. Some will be obvious, and others less so, primarily because they take longer to affect your customers and your business. Misguided cost reduction efforts cause contracts not to be renewed and customers to leave you over time. The result is a never-ending spiral of cost reduction, just to stay afloat. Taking what follows into account should limit the risk of this happening in your company.

The 'Golden rule of cost reduction'
Over the many years I have worked on cost reduction, I have learned there is a single 'Golden Rule' that is the best indicator of future success for major cost-reduction initiatives: *Those doing the implementation have to also do the planning.* Every other approach leads to delays or non-achievement of the objectives.

The other Golden Rule

### Making the Golden Rule work is difficult

Unfortunately, the Golden Rule is rarely put into practice. The single most common reason for this is that cost-reduction efforts involving layoffs are considered to be corporate secrets until actually announced. A plan is still needed, and the plan is put together by external consultants or managers with a limited understanding of the impact of the cost reductions. There is a human tendency to believe that other people's work areas are far less complex than one's own, so it is easy to get management support for reductions in other managers' spending and resources. The planning process usually involves selecting names of people who will actually lead the work. These people are generally not consulted before the announcements are made. At best, they are told simultaneously. Once they see the plans, they have a natural tendency to reject them as 'not invented here', or more correctly 'not invented by me'.

## Clean Rooms

The only solution I have seen work for this is to establish 'Clean Rooms' before the reduction announcement is made. A person in the Clean Room leaves their normal day job to work on the project full-time. To prevent leaks, that time needs to be relatively short. The entire purpose of the Clean Room is to develop a program plan that is realistic and attach it to realistic savings goals.

The most extreme Clean Room I have seen was for the HP-Compaq merger. A member of the co-founder's family, Walter Hewlett, managed to delay the merger for about six months. This gave us loads of extra time to work out very detailed plans. At its peak, there were 2,000 people in the Clean Room. (The overall population was around 155,000.) The result was outstanding execution of the merger integration plan. When the merger was approved, the names of every single account manager were immediately made known to the sales teams and customers, for example. By implication, this of course meant it was immediately clear which overall account managers had lost their prior jobs. In countries where it was legally possible, everyone who was going to lose their jobs found out quickly.

Clean Room people should be free to communicate openly and honestly with each other. They are also free to ask people outside the Clean Room for the information they need to get their work done. However, they are not to respond to requests for information from people outside the Clean Room.

Yes, employees will know there is some sort of 'special project' going on. You need to be clear about the announcement date. Any required workers' council consultations have to be done under a Non-Disclosure Agreement. The average employee will be paranoid and you can expect most to believe they will lose their jobs. This means the Clean Room period has to be kept as short as conceivably possible. Of course that is also true for the overall reduction initiative. If you have not yet worked out which buildings will close and which people will lose their jobs, you need to give them a date when they will know, and keep to it.

## How to achieve reduction goals

Using consulting companies to advance the golden rule

The following chapter on McKinsey's Overhead Value Analysis shows that it is possible for consulting companies to help put the Golden Rule into practice. The worst possible situation is to have your people start to say "The consultants said we have to do this." That sets the consultants up as the enemy. An effective consulting approach sets up and manages the process, but not the content.

## 3.2   Example - Overhead Value Analysis

Overhead Value Analysis or OVA is rather ancient and excellent McKinsey cost reduction methodology. I first came into contact with it in 1982 and 1983, when working for Blue Bell Apparel, the parent company of the Wrangler brand. Times were suddenly quite tough and the corporation wanted to reduce costs. OVA is no longer mentioned by McKinsey on their website, though it may exist under a different name.

The OVA process

Using OVA was my first and most meaningful experience with a process in which the Golden Rule was applied: "Those who execute have to do the planning." This avoided the all-too-common issue where plans are prepared by one team, passed to another team for implementation, and the second team rejects them, protesting that the first team understands nothing about what they do.

After deciding which overhead functions will be targeted, each team leader is given an overall objective: find ways of reducing the work by 40%. The actual objective is a 15% reduction. McKinsey's experience at the time was that companies who target 40% wind up achieving 15% on average, either because some reductions are too extreme, or because some are really cost shifts, moving work from one department to another.

I continue to admire this design. The 40% target means teams have to think differently about their work, while the underlying 15% real-world goal means that solutions that are quick to implement can be prioritized. This is what happened for us in practice. A little more than 15% savings were achieved while the McKinsey team were engaged. There were additional ideas among the 40% list, such as moving to a smaller distribution center, that took more time, and were achieved up to two years later.

# How to achieve reduction goals

## Who was overhead?

While it may seem odd, the definition we used was not what you might expect. I worked in the leadership team for France, the Benelux and Italy, based in Paris. The team leaders who led the work were explicitly told that they themselves would not be eliminated. Everyone else was overhead, with the exception of the sales people who actually called on customers.

## The first step

After we were all introduced to the program, the first step was the analysis of how everyone spent their day. The methodology was quite clever. It used individual face-to-face interviews. Each person was asked what work they did, what was the output, who received the output, and what proportion of their time was spent on each activity. Everyone's time added up to 100%, no matter how many hours a day they worked. At its simplest level, the output of an individual OVA analysis would look like Exhibit 3.1 today:

## Exhibit 3.1

Overhead Value Analysis for one individual

| Name: | C. Blocher | | |
|---|---|---|---|
| **Work** | **Deliverable** | **Received by** | **% of day** |
| Prepare sales reports | Weekly sales report | N. Sarkosy | 60% |
| Attend sales meetings | Meeting minutes and actions | Sales leadership team | 10% |
| Plan 2018 sales quota | Quota letters | Sales people | 15% |
| Salesforce.com implementation | Actions for SFDC implementation team | SFDC project team | 15% |
| | | Total | 100% |

## The most interesting step

Personally, I found the second step to be the most interesting. We then spoke to the people who received the deliverables mentioned in the tables from the first step. The questions were easy: Do you use the deliverable? How often do you get it? How often do you need it? Who else uses it?

There was one painful example: a person in Italy spent all of her time preparing a weekly sales report. This was printed and sent to the regional sales leader in Paris. When we spoke to him, his answer was "I don't use it.

Is it sent to anyone else?" Unfortunately for the Italian lady's job security, it was not. This had been going on for about two years.

## The 40% reduction goal

The following step was to examine all the work and deliverables, looking for opportunities to reduce them by 40%. The McKinsey team placed the emphasis on trying to completely eliminate all deliverables that were not absolutely necessary, then decreasing the content or frequency of what remained. I found this a realistic approach.

Suggestions were categorized by impact and ease of implementation. Since the true objective was a 15% reduction, things that would make life easier in one department but create additional work in another were quickly eliminated. The 40 to 15 gap also meant that we did not have to pay extreme attention to avoiding different departments proposing the same reduction ideas. There was a little of that, and the targeting method meant that it did not matter.

## Learnings

OVA was my first experience with a major corporate cost-reduction effort. I embraced the process and learned a lot. I also learned what happens in an organization when almost everyone (correctly) feels their job is at risk. New rumors circulated every day. Good people were proactive and got jobs elsewhere, rather than taking the risk of staying.

Only the sales teams were happy, since they were explicitly the ones to benefit from the reductions. Since they were also the people who spoke the most to customers, they were able to keep the customers on our side, and we continued to have the top market share in Europe.

I also learned about the positive power of what I can only call paternalistic management. For example, the division leader, David Hayes, tried his best to find out about the personal situations of each employee who was on the redundancy list, before it was communicated. He learned that one of the Parisian warehouse workers had difficult family circumstances and lived in a small trailer in a trailer park. We found a different person to let go; one who would have an easier time getting a new job in the area. My own personal paranoia made me suggest eliminating my own job, a proposal I accompanied by a request to move to a new green-fields distribution center project in Spain. That experience is a whole other story.

# 3.3 Avoid double counting

"Double-counting? Oh, puhleez!"

"3...6...9...12..."

There is a simple way of avoiding a particularly nasty surprise when planning your reduction work. The surprise comes when you have completed your reduction actions, and realize that you will miss your cost savings goals by a wide margin. This happens all the time, and the reason is a particular type of double counting.

## Double-counting and people costs

The key concept to be aware of is that of 'fully-loaded cost'. When you are planning people reductions, it is human nature to try to minimize the number of people affected. If you are working towards a financial objective, the higher the cost you use per person for your calculations, the fewer people you have to let go. To avoid mistakes, make sure you do not use fully-loaded costs in your calculations. Here are examples of what are in fully-loaded costs above and beyond basic salaries and benefits:

- Real estate costs which may be charged out from a central function. It is quite likely that you will set real estate cost reduction goals separately. If you include real estate cross-charges in your people costs, you will be counting real estate twice. Additionally, bear in mind that reducing the people does not necessarily have any effect on the cost of the space they occupy.

- IT costs have two components. If every employee has a PC or Mac, you save the cost of those client devices. However, the central SAP system they use will still be there and reducing the number of people will probably have no effect on the cost of licensing and operating the SAP software. Ensure you count the PC savings in only one cost bucket, probably the IT bucket.

- Telecommunications costs are usually borne by central IT, and may include employees' home Internet connections as well as a certain amount of private communications on a cell phone you may be providing. If your business is not changing, the number of professional phone calls and their duration may not actually change if you have less people. Again, I suggest counting telecommunications savings only in the IT plan.

When planning people reductions, the cost basis should be 'salary and benefits' only.

# 3.4   Innovative ways HP looked at cost

Mark Hurd introduced a new and effective way of looking at certain costs. The main positive aspect was clarity. There were unintended consequences too, as will be seen.

### Focus on cost per employee

As part of the effort to improve business group control of costs, Mark decided to measure some major central costs in terms of dollars per employee. The best examples are probably real estate and IT costs.

- The total cost of real estate of all types per employee was of the order of $9,000 per employee per year. The goal was to take this to $5,000.
- IT costs per employee, including each employee's PC, were about $5,500 per year, and the goal was about $3,200.

While Mark expected the real estate and IT people to negotiate the changes with the business groups, he was unrelenting in his inspection. If any team looked like falling behind, the inspection frequency was increased. Mark's inspection process was somewhat worse than visiting a dentist who does not use anesthetics.

### Real estate cost reduction benefit

I suppose it all came home to me in a colleague's car in Milan. He had kindly picked me up at my hotel close to Linate airport and was driving me to the HP office in suburban Cernusco sul Naviglio. We were passing the spectacular new and shiny IBM office close to the airport. My colleague said, "I just love that building." I mistakenly thought I was about to hear yet another person whining about how much nicer our competitors' offices were than ours. I asked why, with a sigh. He replied, "It puts about 3% extra onto every bid they make, compared to us."

# How to achieve reduction goals

I felt that was the high point of several years of working on cost reduction under Mark Hurd's leadership. In itself, cost reduction is not strategic. What you do with the money is. My Italian colleague was a salesman. Everyone in the company understood that one of the main things we were doing with the money we saved was doubling our sales team. Since the sales people themselves did not feel threatened by all the changes, they were first to understand the positive aspects.

Four real estate cost reduction principles were both clear and problematic.

1. The first was that offices that were close to each other should be combined at the lower-cost location, or combined and moved to an even lower-cost location. At the start, a distance rule was set for this. However, since cities such as Cairo, Moscow, Lagos and Istanbul have disastrous traffic at almost all times of day, the distance principle had to be changed to a travel time principle. Naturally, the new distances to some combined offices were not realistic for everyone, so some resigned as soon as they could find other jobs with a more reasonable commute time.

2. Offices with less than a certain number of employees were to be closed, provided they were not the only office in a particular country. Exceptions had to be made, though they were very difficult indeed to obtain. Two examples were both for customer-specific petroleum industry sites, one in Russia and one in Saudi Arabia. If the sites had been closed, employees would have had long air travel to work from the closest remaining office. It was also considered acceptable for people to work from home. While this may seem reasonable to the eye of someone from North America or Western Europe, 'home' is a multi-generational extended family concept in many other countries, and working from home was not realistic.

3. A company was hired to inspect the amount of time each desk was occupied in the larger offices. Naturally, sales people spent the majority of their time with customers, as did field service engineers. There were also times of the week where less people were found to be in many offices, such as late on Friday afternoons. An overall calculation was made and the result was that less space and desks

were made available than the number of employees. The main problem with this quickly became evident in large sales offices like the one in the City of London. While sales people spent most of their time away from the office, they all wanted to be there simultaneously first thing on Monday mornings. Since there was not enough desk space, people visiting the office at such times were greeted by the spectacle of employees sitting on the floor doing the email and other administration.

4.   Office space costs in different parts of cities were analyzed in detail. In many cases, we moved from city-center offices to ones in less expensive suburban locations. Sometimes, such as in Paris, we did not have to move far for the cost difference to be substantial.

## Surprising amounts of space in some locations

I had my first visit to the corporate HQ in Palo Alto while all of this was going on. I was struck by the fact that there were no shared desks and that everyone appeared to have loads of space, compared to what I had seen elsewhere. There also seemed to be relatively few people in the office, as anyone who could avoid a nasty daily commute on highway 101 was happy to stay at home, now that was encouraged.

A milder version of the same phenomenon was also visible in the EMEA HQ in Geneva, where we do not have the same traffic challenges. It turned out that this was not as odd as you might think. The Palo Alto and Geneva buildings were owned by HP, were among the oldest buildings in the corporation, and were fully amortized. This meant their cost per employee was far lower than the goal for the corporation, despite being located in places with among the highest real estate costs in the world. Since this was not intuitive, it created a perception problem: visitors from locations that were being reduced or eliminated believed the HQ people were not applying the same rules to themselves.

## One odd real estate decision

When an average amount of space was calculated per employee, it was done exactly as described: per employee. No space was foreseen for temporary contractors, despite the plan that they should represent about a quarter of the workforce. This exacerbated the space problems in the crowded locations, and pressured many more people to work at home.

## Consequences of the real estate decisions

On the positive side, the costs did indeed go down, and the objectives were achieved, quickly followed by the setting of even more aggressive objectives. On the negative side, I feel the real estate initiatives damaged the social fabric of the company. You never really knew whether your colleagues would be coming into the office on any particular day. Social events that used to be common essentially disappeared. The HP employee pride in our brand decreased, and this was evident in our annual employee survey results. Fortunately for the business, employee happiness does not have much effect on customer happiness, and the HP businesses continued to do well.

## IT cost reduction for end users

While most of the decisions about reducing IT cost made perfect sense, one was particularly silly. Prior to Mark Hurd's arrival, we had implemented central IT teams for end users on each site. They were justified based on expertise, meaning they could solve problems far more quickly than people could on their own. To pick an example of the work they did, each employee received a new PC every two to three years. The central help desk set up the new PCs in batches, sometimes setting up as many as ten PCs at the same time. Since they did lots of this, they were very good at it. The actual amount of work for them averaged 20 to 30 minutes per PC. Meanwhile, the employees continued to work with their old PCs.

This work was eliminated in IT, and each employee had to learn to set up his or her own PC. Since it happened rarely, none of us were very good at it. It became a standard and acceptable excuse to tell your colleagues that you would be spending a full day setting up your new PC and moving the files from the old PC to the new one, doing nothing else for that day. Since we were not good at it, and there was no local support, we then interrupted our colleagues regularly to ask for advice. This, in my personal opinion, was the single decision that had the most widespread negative consequences. The central IT function achieved their cost goals essentially by transferring twenty times the PC setup costs to the other businesses and functions. (Please don't do anything like this.) While that initial decision was partially reversed some three years after Mark Hurd's departure, it is still largely in place.

## Three corporate data centers

Randy Mott took over as head of IT shortly after Mark Hurd started as CEO. Randy lived near Austin Texas, and had been head of IT at Dell and Walmart. He decided to centralize our internal data centers, moving from more than 100 to just three. If you were going to choose where to put a data center, you would probably understand that cooling costs are a major decision factor, and choose a location like northern Canada, if everything else were equal. He chose Austin, Houston and Atlanta. Still, the real estate costs were low in the three locations, offsetting some of the additional energy costs. I should add that I have no knowledge of any financial incentives the states of Texas and Georgia may have added into the mix.

On a side note, when I worked with a consultancy company who provided advice on locations for distribution warehouses many years ago, it became obvious that the key local person's home town was always close to the top of the selection list. For example, when DEC chose its main spare parts and repair hub for Europe, the person who had the decision was a native of the city of Nijmegen in eastern Holland. By amazing coincidence, Nijmegen was the top city on the list of suggestions the consultants provided. I suppose it is human nature to choose a location you know well, if it is at least a reasonable choice. For the record, Nijmegen was a perfect location, and I am sure other Dutch cities on the major highways would also have been equally good choices. The attractive way the Dutch government taxed import / export companies meant that no other European country could have been considered.

## Unintended consequences of three corporate data centers

There was some balloon squeezing. By this I mean that many of the pre-existing data centers for internal HP use also hosted computer equipment for contracts where we operated customer data centers. When corporate IT moved out of these buildings, the outsourcing business was left with the choice of paying the full cost of the building or engaging in the highly disruptive process of moving the customers' equipment. In general, they had to stay where they were, and simply be less profitable. Once the corporate IT team had committed the savings to Mark Hurd, there was no way back. Please don't make this mistake in your own data center consolidation efforts.

## Elimination of 'shadow IT'

To move from over a thousand business applications to a more reasonable number, all so-called 'shadow IT' was eliminated. Shadow IT was applications and servers that different departments bought and operated on their own. The so-called Y2K challenge, ensuring that all systems could deal with four-digit year numbers when we reached the year 2000, had already shown that fragmented IT was problematic. In 2017, the security imperatives would be obvious, but they were less so in 2006. In any case the locally owned hardware and software were eliminated. The applications were often critical to the success of the teams concerned, and the centralized team was not always able to replace them with something useful.

I suppose one consequence was a rise in amazing Excel skills. Some truly fabulous solutions were developed using Excel, Access, and even Word macros. I feel a shadow IT elimination initiative would be far less successful today. The existence of cloud computing means that many locally developed solutions would simply be replaced by SaaS offerings from third parties. As it was, when we went through the exercise there were some automated processes which simply became manual.

## Watch out for exchange rates

All objectives were set in US dollars. This is of course appropriate for a company whose accounting is reported to Wall Street in dollars. However, most of the business was outside the USA, so the costs were not in dollars. We went through a period where the dollar rose significantly against other currencies, making the cost objectives much harder to achieve. No change was made to the objectives, so we had to plan additional reductions of people and other costs to meet them. When currencies moved in ways that were more favorable, the objectives were not changed either, creating a local perception of unfairness. If you are setting cost reduction objectives for different countries around the world, I recommend setting them in local currency at the start, and not changing them, no matter what exchange rate fluctuations you encounter. Inflation rates have been low in most countries for quite a long time, so are generally not worth worrying about.

## Effect of manufacturing outsourcing on average real estate costs

Until 2016, HP used a common practice when charging real estate costs to the businesses and functions occupying the space. An overall average was calculated and the same number was used for everyone. In reality, hardware manufacturing sites had the lowest real estate costs. We moved some manufacturing to subcontractors in China and elsewhere, and laid off the corresponding HP employees. This meant that the average real estate cost per square foot / meter for the remaining employees went up, making the target numbers harder to achieve.

## 'Sale and leaseback' is not less expensive

Moving to the '0.5' category of cost savings, we decided to sell and lease back our buildings in a number of locations, including some where they had been fully amortized. This moves a cost from the Balance Sheet to the P&L. It also moves cash flow from your company to whoever is the new owner of your building. I realize many technical finance people are obsessed by ROIC (Return on Invested Capital) and its supposed correlation to stock price, but remain unconvinced. Sale and leaseback makes your operating profit objectives harder to achieve.

## 3.5 Presenting HP's approach to customers

Once it became clear that the cost saving approach was successful and seemed to have a positive effect on our stock price, major HP customers wanted to know more. I presented the initiatives to several customers.

### One memorable presentation

While presentations to 'normal' companies went as expected, with a high level of interest, there was a category of company where my information was received differently, to say the least. These were former state monopolies in areas like telecommunications and electricity. I was particularly fascinated by one presentation to a corporate leadership team. Unfortunately, I feel I cannot name them, as it would still be embarrassing for all concerned, or at least I hope so. The context was that their new competitors were selling at prices that made the former state monopoly unprofitable. We were trying to sell them some solutions to reduce their IT costs, and that part of the discussion went quite well. I covered all of the other initiatives too. My presentation style was to focus on their competition for each point. For example, I asked about their average cost per employee, and the CFO knew the number. She had never thought about their competitors' costs per employee, and was at least receptive to the idea that she should find out.

### Real estate

Things went downhill when I covered real estate costs per employee. We were sitting in an exotic conference room in the part of the major city that had the very highest office space costs in the country. Their new competitors were all in the low-cost suburbs of the same city. The team saw no problem with this at all. "This is our HQ so we can't move it." "This building is an important part of our brand." "The building is in our advertising." There was absolutely no way to persuade them that they would have to address it to become profitable. It was just an untouchable.

## Presenting HP's approach to customers

Cost per employee

Some of their costs were typical of those faced in generous state-owned companies where the tax payers have traditionally funded longer vacations and earlier retirement ages than they receive themselves. Airlines like Air France and Lufthansa have found these benefits extremely difficult to change in the face of low-cost carriers. The only approach that seems to have any chance of working in these unionized environments is to maintain the benefits for existing employees, and to give less attractive benefits that match the competitors' benefits to the new hires.

It is still a very tough negotiation, and Lufthansa has had quite a number of strikes about exactly this. Meanwhile Ryanair and EasyJet continue to grow. My presentation on costs per employee went this way too, and the leadership team felt my suggestions were not negotiable with their unions. I did not realize at the time that two of the leadership team were in the union themselves. I would not have changed what I said, but would have found their reactions easier to understand.

Mental gymnastics sometimes needed

While privatization had happened some years before my session, it was clear to me that the leadership team had not adjusted to the world of competition. If they could not become profitable quickly because the real estate and employee contract changes were unpalatable, that was "just too bad", and they would have to wait a few more years. They had all spent their entire careers with a single employer and did not have a comprehensive view of the business world in general, and the nature of competition in particular.

The final proof happened as I was leaving. One of them was beside me, taking me to reception. Three others were some way behind, walking along the same empty corridor. I overheard one of them saying "I understand what he is saying, but I am really overloaded and can't work on it. I haven't even been able to take all my sick days this year." If your company leaders think 'sick days' are an employee benefit you are all entitled to take as vacation days, you really have a whole other set of problems.

# 3.6   Manage people reductions by geography

While it may be tempting for a multinational to give businesses and functions total control over their people reductions, this is not practical.

## Reductions must be coordinated

From an internal perspective, multinational companies have both geographic and organizational dimensions. You may have several business units that are managed individually, as well as corporate functions such as Finance that report centrally. The business and functional teams only come together at the corporate headquarters level. Your CEO may have told each business and functional leader that he / she is fully in charge of their area and 100% responsible for its results. When it comes to involuntary people and indeed other reductions spread around the world, this principle cannot possibly apply. In short, the internal reason is that people in each location, for example your subsidiary in Germany, will talk to each other over lunch or socially outside work. If one business or function announces that its team will have layoffs or will move to a less expensive building, all of the other teams will immediately want to know what is happening to them. If the other teams are not ready to communicate, business will be disrupted and your customers will suffer. In the absence of any communication, they will assume the worst.

## Regulations vary by geography

Quite apart from the risk of organizational paranoia and slowdown, regulations about letting people go are entirely geographical. In most countries, a single set of laws apply. Some countries are federations and have laws that differ by state. It is quite common that you have a single opportunity to announce layoffs for your company in a given time period, for example a year, and that nothing further can be done in that time. Your working assumption must be that such regulations exist everywhere. It is therefore essential that the central planning team ensures that all businesses and functions work to a single announcement calendar per country. This does of course have implications for overall timing, as you will be constrained by the team that needs the longest to be ready.

A result of the legal situation is that you will not be able to do what you want when you want. In particular, you should plan on making people reductions voluntary in France, Germany, Spain, the Netherlands, Belgium and indeed a number of other countries. There are so many legal and process constraints involved with layoffs that they quickly become impractical. Of course, if you were hoping to use involuntary layoffs to get rid of relatively poor performers or people with above-average salaries, you won't be able to do that. Your star performers may take the attractive packages on offer and simply go to one of your competitors. I suggest the selective use of retention bonuses for the very few people you absolutely want to keep. Commit to give them a substantial proportion of their salary as a one-time payment after 18 months, for example.

The nature and regulations about how employees must be represented vary widely by geography. Europe has supra-national regulations in addition to local rules. The next chapter covers guidelines on how to incorporate this environment into your plans.

## Your strategy should differ by country

Mark Hurd had some great guidance on how corporate business strategies need to vary by country. I happened to find myself on my own with him in a meeting room in a hotel in Nice, late one evening. I had just started to represent EMEA on the HP corporate strategy team. My question to Mark was "Since we have a single corporate strategy, what can I do that would actually be useful in EMEA?" His answer was instructive. "The people on my team will push every country in the world to do everything. That makes no sense. We can probably only implement every single thing in one country: The United States. I want you to work with country leadership teams to give them a single acceptable method of determining which subset of the corporate strategy will generate the most operating profit in their country. The answer will depend on the customers and competitors in each country, for example. Then when my staff come and tell them to do something that makes no sense locally, they will be able to push back in a logical and consistent way."

The message here is that companies need to accept that not every cost reduction tactic is appropriate in every country. Set out the criteria for acceptable pushback. For example, if your overall objective is a 20% cost reduction, do you really want to force a smaller country that is growing at 35% annually to put that aside for a moment and fire people?

# 3.7 Working with Workers' Councils

Achieving cost reductions in most European countries means working with employee representatives, usually referred to as Workers' Councils.

## History

Workers' councils have quite a long and varied history, associated with communism in Russia and with the rise in the power of employee unions in other countries. I will use France as a reasonably good example of how the system works. Workers' Councils often make the news in France, where their strike actions attract international media attention. The laws governing them date from 1945, and oblige the owners of any company with 50 employees or more to organize the election of employee representatives. Above a certain number of people, executives have to be represented as well.

## Two election rounds

The French system has two election rounds. The first is open exclusively to union members. Anyone can propose themselves as a candidate in the second round. However, if more than half the employees vote in the first round and enough people have been elected, there is no second round. There are a lot of other details that vary depending on the size of the company. For example, a formal union representative must be chosen by a union and will be the sole representative of that union for any company of less than 300 employees. The union representative cannot be elected and does not count against the number of people who must be elected. The union delegate has the right to be in all meetings and must be consulted. Most workers' councils are legally required to meet monthly. In companies the size of HP, workers' council members may work full-time as employee representatives, entirely at the expense of the company. This is also the case in some other countries.

# How to achieve reduction goals

## Consultation versus co-determination

While a company can agree something more restrictive, workers' councils are consultative bodies in the majority of European countries. This means that you absolutely must inform the council of forthcoming business decisions that affect the employees, and listen to them. However, you do not have to take the advice they offer. In some countries, such as Belgium, 'co-determination' tends to be the rule. What that means is that you must reach agreement with the council, and cannot move forward without it. It is critical to understand whether you are in a consultative or co-determination situation in each country.

## My first experience in France

I moved to Mulhouse, France, in 1979. The Wrangler parent company had acquired two production factories in Alsace, and I was one of two engineers assigned to bring standard corporate production and incentive processes to the team. I found the process quite surprising, to say the least. The concept of piece work already existed, and moving them to a 'straight line' incentive system was well accepted. (This means, for example, if you produce double the volume, you get double the pay.) Other things were quite odd. My favorite example involves a communist union member and the weights pregnant women were allowed to carry. Madame Liotta was an Italian member of the CGT union, closely associated with the French communist party, which was still strong at the time, and about to enter a coalition government. She was quite well off, and tended to mainly come into work on the days we were holding the Workers' Council meetings. As we set up the new work processes, I had read absolutely every conceivable regulation about working conditions.

On the day in question, I was asked to come to the Workers' Council meeting to cover the "unacceptable" weights we were asking pregnant women to lift. I understood the regulations in detail. Women were generally limited to lifting 16 kilos (35 lbs.) and pregnant women could lift no more than 11 kilos. I had made certain there was nothing to lift that weighed more than 10 kilos in the entire factory. "But" said Madame Liotta, "if I am a pregnant woman, I lift more than one of these stacks of cloth per day. If it weighs 10 kilos, and I lift 20 of them in a day, that's 200 kilos. It is totally illegal!" I have to say that the plant manager and I left the room at that point as we did not want to explode in public. The negotiations at the time were full of silliness like that.

Unfortunately, our parent company was anti-union and had no tolerance for this sort of thing. A year or so after I left Mulhouse, the two unions (CFDT and CGT) went on strike, each demanding that the company no longer recognize the other union. The consequence was a corporate decision to shut down the two factories, which were among the best performers in the company. I suppose the lowering of trade barriers with China, Vietnam, Bangladesh and other low-cost countries was inevitable, and they would have gone the way of almost all other clothing manufacturing in Europe and North America sooner or later.

### Denmark sales plan changes, rules in Morocco

There are individual countries that have regulations you need to understand and deal with. In Denmark, HP had to give six-month advance notification of any change to sales compensation plans for example. I am not picking on Denmark. Morocco, like some other former French colonies, copied French labor law some time ago, and has not copied the changes France introduced in the last few years to introduce a little flexibility. One of my former senior colleagues is based in Morocco and had a role covering all of Africa. He was told his job was being eliminated. His reaction may seem surprising: "Fantastic, when can I leave?" The person giving him the news did not realize that he was entitled to receive two months of pay per year worked, and there was no budget for it. My colleague is still there, with a different job, though he has understood that he is not really wanted. The point is that you can't make any assumptions about what is easy or difficult, and must investigate the rules in each country in detail.

### European Works Councils

Since 1994, all companies with over 1,000 employees, and with at least 150 in each of two countries, are required to allow the election of a European Works Council (EWC) for their employees. If an employer does not initiate the process, a request from at least 100 employees launches it. These councils are consultative in nature. HP worked well with their Council and

# How to achieve reduction goals

I presented major changes to them a number of times. You are required to consult with your European Works Council first, then at local level. While regular meetings are scheduled, you can also call a special one for a particular event.

## One tactic I found helpful

I get nervous when speaking to large groups and deal with this by over-preparing. The European Works Council meetings were something I found stressful, particularly if I had to present something that I knew would be perceived as negative, meaning layoffs. While the EWC is a consultative body and their agreement is not required, they do have to formally agree that the relevant consultations have taken place. A certain format has to be respected, and answers must be provided to all questions asked. The stress level is not helped by the fact that the delegates are allowed to speak in their own languages, and your company has to provide interpreters.

The meetings always lasted two days. The attendees on the first day were the EWC members and HP's HR people who managed the process. Business leaders' sessions were on the second day, and a joint dinner was held on the first evening. The single over-preparation tactic I found most helpful was to find out who was being the most aggressive during the first day, and to sit beside that person at dinner. I was fortunate in that the most aggressive person usually happened to be French, where rhetoric has high cultural value, and I speak French. The dinner dialog always meant that I was able to establish a certain level of mutual trust, if not agreement. My presentation sessions on the second day tended to attract less emotion than those of some of my colleagues.

## The one thing you should never do

I have never seen any successful attempt at short-cutting the consultation process. I have seen a number of failed attempts, each of which shared some common attributes. Typically, a business leader discovers that he or she has committed to cost saving numbers that are not compatible with the European consultation requirements. Where that leader decides to intervene, they are usually a US-based manager with no European experience. "We are totally committed to our cost reduction numbers this quarter. I will go and sort out these Europeans. They just want to delay things." These interventions have always been counter-productive, delaying or preventing success.

"Bonjour, mes amis, there's a new sheriff in town!"

Build it into your plan

The message here is clear. You will not be able to change the consultation processes and will need to build them into your plans. Misguided attempts to cut corners usually delay implementation. The regulations evolve constantly, and rules you experienced several years ago may no longer apply. Some new European Union members in Central Europe have been copying the French and German practices, so you should expect similar processes there too.

There will be countries where involuntary people reductions are going to be difficult or impossible while the overall parent company is profitable. Understand which ones, and plan on it. Planning means setting aside the budget necessary for voluntary departures. Lack of correct planning has unpleasant consequences where savings numbers have been committed to investors without the necessary investigation of what is actually possible. The main consequence I have seen is that the people reduction targets get increased in the low-regulation countries, such as the USA, even where the additional reductions put customers and business at risk. Please be careful and plan appropriately.

# 3.8 Reducing capital costs

Corporate financing costs can be improved by having less capital tied up in your company. Some methods of doing this are risky in that they may negatively impact customers. Others are customer-neutral.

## Change supplier Ts&Cs

While it can cause cash flow issues for your suppliers, another way of reducing your costs is to unilaterally decide to pay your suppliers later than you currently do. Indeed, if you can get into a situation where you pay your suppliers after your customers pay you, your company may not need much working capital at all. Each country seems to have a cultural norm for how quickly suppliers are paid. 15 days is sometimes seen in Finland, and government bodies tend to favor 90 and even 120 days in Italy, for example. The point here is that there is no hard and fast rule. If you are a large company, you can impose whatever you want, within reason. Unless your suppliers also happen to be your customers, it is difficult to see how changing payment terms can have a negative customer impact. There is a way to help your suppliers offset the negative impact the change will have for them.

As a starting point, I suggest trying to standardize on 90-day payment terms. The point at which the 90 days start is also important. It does not have to be the day on which the supplier receives the invoice. Test using the 15th of each month, or the last day of each month as the reference, for example. Don't expect suppliers to like it if you have been more generous up to now, and expect them to hate it if you are the worst payer in the market. They are of course free not to bid for your business, and that may result in higher costs at your end. I therefore recommend testing in one or two markets before you do a full roll-out. After all, suppliers have power in some markets, and you need them. One way to mitigate the financial impact for suppliers is to use intermediaries like Tungsten. Suppliers issue invoices using Tungsten's systems, and Tungsten passes them on to client companies after validation. If a supplier wants to be paid immediately, Tungsten pays them, and keeps a percentage of the final amount paid by the company placing the order. This is simply a variety of what is known as a factoring process.

'Free On Board' designates the location at which goods are transferred from a supplier to your company. Any good procurement department should understand this and use it as a point of negotiation. Let's suppose your business buys a lot of something relatively heavy that is manufactured in Shenzen in China and needed by you in Hamburg, Germany. The average shipping time by sea is 28 days. If you buy FOB Shenzen, the goods are on your books while at sea, and on the supplier's books if you buy FOB Hamburg. Suppliers also understand this. A fair negotiation would involve sharing information about your and their cost of capital and working out which one saves the most money. If costs of capital mean FOB Shenzen is the best mutual arrangement, you should be able to get a small price break for agreeing to it.

Inventory

"Let's just reduce our inventory by 30%" sounds intelligent without a discussion of the potential impact on customers and on the rest of your company. Inventory reduction needs to be accompanied by carefully chosen metrics to ensure there is no negative impact on customers. As always, the metric standard and baseline need to be established before you change inventory levels. The two most common and relevant metrics are:

- Deliver to first commit: your ability to promise a specific delivery date to a customer and then meet that delivery date. A sensible definition will also say what is meant by delivery, specifically for the case where multiple items are ordered together. Does the term 'delivery date' refer to the first item delivered, or to the complete order, if you have to split delivery into multiple parts. The only sensible answer is that it has to refer to the complete order. After all, the last thing you deliver may be required to make the other items function. Please do not fall into the trap of a metric that states that incomplete delivery is OK.

# Reducing capital costs

- Level of fill: the proportion of the line items on an order that are delivered by the commit date, or indeed at all. For example, if a customer orders 20 different items and you deliver 19 on time, that is usually a 95% level of fill. Level of fill gets complicated by rules about partial delivery of individual line items. If a customer orders 10 pieces of wood and 500 nails, you need to ensure that your metric considers that not delivering 10 nails has different consequences to not delivering the 10 pieces of wood. I suggest only counting complete line items. In this example, delivering 490 nails would have the same impact on your metric as delivering no nails at all.

When reporting progress on inventory reduction, always report the service level metrics at the same time. Nobody should feel good about reducing inventory at the expense of customers.

## Consider channel inventory

Playing around with distributor or reseller inventory falls firmly into the '0.5' category of cost reduction. Most companies that use resellers count anything shipped to the resellers as sold, whether or not the reseller has sold it on to an end customer. This is a risky practice if your reseller Ts&Cs state that you will take back unsold inventory without penalty, at any time. Yes, it is possible to work with your resellers to agree that their default level of stock should be increased, for example from 30 days of expected sales to 45 days.

If you go ahead with this plan, you reduce the inventory on your books by 15 days, but put costs up in your channel. It is of course most tempting to make such changes just before the end of your fiscal year, improving your results, particularly if you count the 15 days of inventory that has been transferred as 'sold'. This tactic will be quite obvious to your resellers and they will feel equally entitled to transfer inventory back to you as it suits their financial reporting. In short, I feel this is a game that is not worth playing. It does not represent a real cost saving unless the total inventory held by both you and your resellers goes down.

# How to achieve reduction goals

## Change customer Ts&Cs

Beware changing customer Ts&Cs when your competitors are not making the same changes! Local car dealer André Chevalley changed a policy a few years back and it lost them business. My wife and I had bought four cars there over the years. When picking her car up from its routine service visit, the service receptionist told her "Sorry, but we don't send invoices anymore. You must pay right away. Some people have not been paying their bills on time."

We had been used to receiving the bill at home and having a month to pay. My wife asked, quite simply "Have I myself ever paid late?" The answer was "We have to have the same rule for everyone. Chasing people to pay costs us too much." Well, deciding they did not want to chase the tiny fraction of people who paid late lost them a lot more business. It was the easiest of decisions to be disloyal and buy our following car from their main competitor.

## Zalando example of flexible customer Ts&Cs

Zappos is legendary for good service in the USA, and Zalando has copied a lot of their business model in Europe. It is a web-based business. When you start with them, you need to pay by credit card when you order, though returns are free of charge, including carriage. After you have built up a history with them, they give you the choice of having an invoice, payable after 15 days, and up to a certain amount. Once they see that you pay on time, the limit for pay-later invoicing is gradually raised.

This is an excellent way of having the most attractive Ts&Cs be directed at the customers who deserve them. It is similar to the approach of supermarkets that use self-scanning checkouts to save money. If your first random check shows that you have not made any mistakes, your second check will probably be quite some time later. The frequency of checks depends on how good you are at doing the work they transferred to you.

# 3.9   Reducing sales costs

It is always risky to change your sales model or sales coverage density. It can seem intelligent when examined superficially, less so when considering the details. Here are some mistakes I have seen, including some I may have made while responsible for HP's Sales Strategy and Operations team in EMEA.

### Think outside your company

First and foremost, remember that you are competing with other companies for your customers' business. Any changes you make to sales models will affect your win rates. Indeed, your win rate can drop to zero if you simply decide that you are not going to show up at all when business is on offer. I have never seen this simple fact considered correctly when evaluating sales model changes. By this I mean it is often an item on a spreadsheet, but the underlying assumptions have never been realistic.

Unfortunately, I have to say that some of this lack of realism happened on my watch. In short, in all too many cases, we assumed we could preserve or even improve win rates while assigning fewer sales people or sales hours to a customer. It should be obvious that if you change, and your competitors do not, your win rate will change, up or down. Think about what would happen if you moved to telesales, or selling via Skype conferences, and your competitors continue to send sales people on site...

Time and time again, when I or people in my team interviewed senior executives of our largest customers, they prioritized one thing: having a single sales person to talk to who would be responsible for everything HP sold. That is impossible to achieve by telesales. Customers expect senior sales people to understand the customer's industry and business in detail. I just can't see how that can be done without frequent visits to the customer's site, and meetings with senior leaders. Some of the most upset customers I met were those who had such sales people, then lost them as we tried to reduce cost. We generally lost share to competitors who continued to operate the model we abandoned.

"John, Mary, is someone else there with you? Do not listen to that man, repeat, do not..."

### Ensure your cost comparison is correct

Generally Accepted Accounting Practices (GAAP) mean that it is easy to draw entirely incorrect conclusions when comparing sales models. The most common mistake happens when companies sell direct to some customers and also use resellers for others. Please read what follows carefully. It requires few words to explain, but some time to understand:

*When your own sales people sell, the cost is accounted for in your 'Selling, General and Administrative costs', considered to be 'Below the line' costs in most accounting systems. When your resellers sell, the main way they are compensated for selling is through 'channel rebates'; discounts from your list prices. These discounts do not appear in your P&L, Balance Sheet or Cash Flow statements at all.*

# Reducing sales costs

Channel or reseller rebates are considered to be 'contra revenue', and are not in your P&L according to standard accounting practices in most countries. What this means is that when companies compare the costs of selling direct and indirect, they tend to look at cost lines that are in their accounts somewhere. They latch on to items like 'Cooperative marketing funding' that are indeed in their P&L. They then come to the entirely wrong conclusion that selling via resellers only costs a fraction of the cost of selling direct. To do the cost comparison correctly, you need to include the channel rebate in the analysis. This is totally logical, because the rebate is what you pay distributors and resellers to sell for you.

## Benchmarks

Consulting companies that provide cost benchmarks never take the direct / indirect factor into account, and never talk about channel rebates in my experience. You are left to draw your own conclusions, and that is difficult to do well. Be very careful if you are using such benchmarks as a basis for your decisions.

## Comparing costs of sales specialists and generalists

Where corporations sell complex products and services to large customers, they tend to use a combination of generalist and specialist sales people. The generalist is supposed to have a deep understanding of the customer, the customer's industry, and the investments customers should make to improve their chances of gaining market share. The specialists have a deep understanding of your company's product or service, but know relatively little about the customer or their industry. The two types of sales people win by working together.

In matrixed organizations, the specialists probably belong to product business units, and the generalists to a separate sales organization. When cost pressures arrive, the business unit managers often say "Why do I need to pay the generalists? I am already paying the specialists. Let's get rid of the entire generalist sales force." I am not making this type of thing up. This was an HP Executive Vice-President's argument when he led a product business group at HP and it led to the elimination of the separate global sales team. Unfortunately, it also led to losing many of the deals that depended on understanding the customer and their industry in detail. There were and still are enough pure specification-based procurement deals to keep the hardware business going, but the decision was short-sighted, and has since been reversed. The key point here is that our competitors did not make similar changes, and then gained share for knowledge-based deals when we changed our sales model. Cisco was probably the biggest beneficiary.

### The importance of generalists for large customers

The Gartner-owned Research Board has about 260 current and former Fortune Global 500 CIOs as members. They publish an annual survey of their members' opinions about their largest IT suppliers. My own analysis of the data shows that the single most important factor that drives their overall ratings is the existence of a single sales person responsible for all business with the customer. If your company decides it does not need sales generalists, please bear this in mind, and remember that your competitors will probably not be making the same decision.

### Correctly comparing sales costs for big and small customers

If your company has some very large customers, the sales efficiency for these customers is usually far better than for smaller customers. The primary reason for this is that the majority of this substantial revenue comes from the renewal of existing agreements, requiring little effort. An ideal cost comparison should use these two guidelines:

1. As a starting point, assume that renewing existing deals takes 10% of the effort required to bring in new business. Adjust the 10% number if you have better data for your own business.
2. Don't compare revenue by sales person. Ideally, you should compare two things, one negative and one positive. First, compare the discounts from list price. Large customers usually get greater discounts. Then compare operating profit or at least gross margin by customer. A dollar of discount from list price has exactly the same value as a dollar of operating profit. The greater discounts often counter-balance the lower revenue numbers from smaller customers. However, the discounts are 'contra revenue', and are therefore not

in standard P&L statements, so many companies do not include them in their cost comparisons.

## Comparing sales models is difficult

It is more difficult than you might expect to make fair comparisons between the costs of different sales models. It can be done, and is worth the effort. Bear in mind that changes you make to your sales models will take some time to have an effect. Meanwhile, your competitors will keep selling with their current models, and will do their best to take share from you.

## Decreasing sales costs by 'nudging'

We all want our customers to have the best possible experience with our products and services. In many cases, that involves giving them the choice of additional products or services when they buy something. In the interests of cost reduction, you want to make the additions part of a single sales motion, rather than requiring a new selling effort. In their book *Nudge*[4], Thaler and Sunstein refer to the process as "benevolent paternalism." The issue they address is simple. Customers who are presented with multiple choices often choose nothing at all. The solution is to 'benevolently' preselect optimal choices for the customer. The customer needs to be able to opt out from the preselections, and the whole process is quite easy to abuse.

## Good and bad examples of nudging

To pick a negative example, preselecting an extended warranty offering when a customer buys a home appliance at retail is almost never in the customer's best interest. However, extending the standard warranty from 12 months to 36 may be a great risk-reduction option for a car, where repairs can cost a lot. Benevolent paternalism would suggest that the extended warranty proposal should be made with every new car sale. That saves the cost of going back to the customer to try to sell it at the end of the standard warranty period.

---

[4]  Richard H. Thaler and Cass R. Sunstein: *Nudge*, Penguin, 2008, 2009, ISBN 978-0-14-311526-7

## How to achieve reduction goals

In countries where it is legal to do so, 'evergreen' automatically-renewing service contracts are good idea, and will eliminate the need of a customer discovering they are no longer entitled to a service they need. A positive example would be a software support contract that includes rights to use new versions as well as access to telephone support. An example of non-benevolent auto-renewals is the practice of many fitness clubs of renewing memberships automatically, unless three months' advance notice of termination is given. The reason this is often negative is that the clubs renew automatically, even if the person is not actually using their subscription. A benevolent practice would do so only for regular users.

# 3.10 Company cars

"Sure, your car is bigger and fancier, but what are the tax implications?"

While not all that common in the USA, company cars are a routine benefit offered in other countries. The reason is tax treatment. Some countries do not tax employees on the benefit. Others limit the amount that can be deducted, or require itemized (though not easily verifiable) lists of trips for which the car was used.

## Car decisions are quite emotional for some

Cultural attitudes to cars vary, and it is safe to say that Italians, for example, are very attached to their choice of car, particularly Italian men. Change your company car policy at your peril. The level of emotion any change will attract can be so time-consuming to deal with that you should think carefully before deciding it is worth it. Multinational companies based in the USA tend to make less than optimal decisions, without consultation. Sometimes the decisions are driven by emotion, rather than fact. "We don't have company cars here in the United States, so there is no reason to have them anywhere else." Please consider what follows before jumping conclusions.

## Tax impact for employees

Let's suppose the company car deal costs your company $1,000 per month per employee who benefits from it. Let's also suppose that we are talking about a country with a high marginal tax rate of 50%, and that the car benefit is not taxable. This means the car is actually worth at least $2,000 per month to the employee, as he or she would have to earn at least $2,000 to be able to afford to pay $1,000 for it. The point here is that eliminating company cars would cost the affected employees double what it would save your company.

Tax considerations in different countries mean there are countries where company cars are the rule, rather than the exception. If you remove such a substantial benefit, your employees should find it easy to move to another company, keeping the benefit. Is that what you want to happen?

## Is it worth asking the employees?

We thought we had a clever idea about cars during the Wrangler-McKinsey Overhead Value Analysis exercise in France. We had 27 sales people with company cars. We told them we wanted to save money on cars and asked them to work together to decide what car they would like, within the budget number we provided.

We had not thought it through completely. The unanimous answer came back that they wanted us to supply 27 Volkswagen Golf GTIs. However, the largest French distributors and indeed many other clothing stores were very sensitive indeed to the 'Frenchness' of what they were selling. One of our selling points was that we had three manufacturing plants in France, despite being an American company. We decided that we could not send the French sales people out in German cars, so they had to be satisfied with their second choice, the now-defunct Talbot brand. I would like to think that the idea of asking the people to come up with the reduction suggestion was the right one. We should have done a better job of thinking it through completely.

## Reducing the cost

It may well be appropriate to find cheaper options and less expensive suppliers for company cars. Please look closely at each country's situation when you do this. These examples should illustrate the point:

- A certain high-tech company decided (from another country) that their Italian sales people and service engineers should abandon their Italian-brand company cars and be forced to have Škodas. While Škodas are perfectly reliable and comfortable cars from the Czech Republic, the Italians considered this to be a totally unacceptable decision. After about a year of pain and public ridicule, the decision was reversed.
- At HP, we decided that the cost of car lease schemes for executives should be cut, and that was done by reducing choice. In a particular set of countries, if you were an executive, you had to have a particular model of BMW, and in others, it had to be a Mercedes or another brand. Here in Switzerland, BMW was the decision, and the person taking the decision also specified that four-wheel-drive could not be selected as an option, even if the employee was willing to pay for it on their own. The country is covered in snowy Alps. It was quite an effective way of killing the leasing scheme, which had no particular tax benefit. Only people on temporary relocation deals continued to choose the arrangement, and quickly found out that rear-wheel-drive cars are useless on icy mountain roads.
- In the Netherlands, employees were not allowed to select automatic gearboxes for their C-Class Mercedes, even if they had never driven with a manual gearbox in their lives.

These were silly decisions taken by people who did not personally have to live with the consequences.

## Conclusion

Saving money on company car schemes is fraught with problems. It is difficult to get a complete picture of local practices, cultural attitudes to brands, and the employee tax impact of any changes you may want to make in a multinational company. Company car practices differ by country for sound reasons. It would be a mistake to change your policies without understanding the competitive situation and employee consequences in detail for each location.

# 3.11 Reduce number of suppliers

Centralization of procurement of commodity products and services should give substantial negotiation power.

## Mono- and multi-country situations

If you have multiple locations in one country, or indeed multiple locations around the world, it can seem attractive to let the people in charge have total control over everything they buy locally. I see just one advantage to this, though it is substantial. If your procurement is all local, you do a lot of good within your local community, providing jobs that are directly linked to your presence. If you ever need help from the local government, it will be easier to get it. I can see no other advantage to it, assuming you don't count feeding your local people's egos as an advantage. There are many items where you should be able to secure substantial savings by centralizing.

- If your company is reasonably large, IT equipment, particularly PCs and Macs can be obtained more cheaply by signing a single global pricing agreement. Don't assume the US prices are always the lowest. It is safer to agree a uniform percentage discount from the local country list price. Add a clause that guarantees price matching if a local reseller offers even greater discounts.
- Imposing a single standard corporate credit card around the world should mean you get a small percentage of all purchases returned to you by the credit card company. There are two things to watch out for. First, not every card brand is accepted everywhere. American Express charges merchants more than other brands in Europe, and there are entire countries where it is relatively poorly accepted. You may therefore have to accept standardizing on a different brand in some countries. Second, employees who have been using their own cards up to now have probably been accumulating substantial benefits, and they will complain when you remove those benefits. Careful explanation of whose money is being spent is the key.

# How to achieve reduction goals

- Building security and reception services can be put out to global tender. Companies such as Securitas work in most countries around the world.
- You will save a lot of money by having a single global travel service provider manage all travel bookings and adherence to the travel-related part of your corporate expense policy. Once again, there is a disadvantage in that employees will sometimes be able to find lower-priced hotels and air fares. The centralization gives some negotiation power with major airlines and hotel chains, and is worthwhile. Your contract with the service provider should require them to book the lower-priced options that employees may find on their own. Note in passing that the nature of many Airbnb rentals means that employees will not be able to get a receipt that would satisfy tax authorities, so you probably have to exclude use of Airbnb from your potential cost saving list.

In general, I feel that having an 'approved vendor list' will save you a substantial amount of money. Employees will complain about it frequently, and you should probably make exceptions below a certain size of annual spend. Managing this by size of contract does not work, as people who want to get around it just break a large spend up into smaller contracts.

## Example — Eliminating use of business advisory consultants

Eliminating the use of business advisory consultants was one of the first EMEA-wide reduction initiatives I drove at HP. There were challenges, and it required persistence that went way beyond irritating some people

The first issue was to define what such a consultant is and is not. The corporation's perspective was simple: "There is a single corporate business strategy that already exists and will not change for the next few years. There is therefore no conceivable need for anyone to engage a consultant to determine their business strategy."

I must say that it seemed perfectly logical to me. Not so to people who wanted, for example, to determine the size of the healthcare industry in their country and determine how many sales people to hire for it. The corporation's perspective was again simple. "We are saving loads of money so you can hire more sales people. Just get on with the hiring and assign them to the customers who spend the most on IT in your country. If you don't know how much a customer spends on IT, phone the CIO and ask. And by the way, if you are competent, you should already know."

Our procurement systems used codes to identify different types of suppliers. There was a code for 'business advisory consultants', and other codes for other sorts of consultants. The company was spending something like $90 million annually on business advisory consultants, according to the system. The objective was clear. It had to go to $0 within three months.

One thing that was always clear with the reduction objectives at the time was that they would never change. If you, for example, had made a coding mistake and had actually spent your locally reported $2 million on something else, you still had a $2 million reduction objective. As you would expect, the majority of the people spending the $90 million tried to say the consultants were not in fact advising on strategy, but on something else, like how to bid for a particular deal. Mis-classifications also happened in the other direction, so I had to ensure that particular consulting companies' work was micro-inspected and eliminated, no matter how it had been categorized in the systems. I was quite unpopular.

I learned quite a lot about 'balloon squeezing' at the time. In all too-many cases, the official procurement category spend dropped to $0 right away, but the expense had simply been reclassified as something else. This is what led to my 'making it real' approach which required analysis of where savings actually showed up on the formal P&L, balance sheet or cash flow statements.

## Be consistent
Centralizing procurement of items that function together with other items that have not been centralized can cause major issues. It is important to be consistent in your approach, as illustrated by the drawing on the next page.

# How to achieve reduction goals

"So whose bright idea was it to centralize oars?"

# 3.12 Getting better deals from suppliers

Reducing what you pay your suppliers is an essential part of any corporate cost reduction program. It is important that your suppliers continue to be profitable, and several different approaches to achieving a good balance are possible.

## Behavioral economics teachings

In their book *The Why Axis*[5], behavioral economists Uri Gneezy and John List describe their disturbing experiments on how to get the best prices for products and services. All companies have something to learn from this. Here are the salient points from the three most interesting experiments:

## High prices for the handicapped

They took some damaged vehicles to various repair shops. In the control group, people with average physical abilities asked for price quotations for simple body repair work. In the experimental group, the person asking for the quote got out of the vehicle with difficulty and went into the repair shop in a wheelchair to ask for a price. On average, the disabled people received price quotes that were 30 percent higher than the 'normal' men.

The situation was repeated dozens of times with the same results. The researchers' assumption was that the person providing the price quotation assumed that the handicapped customer would not try to get more than one price, and that the able-bodied person would. They tested this in a second experiment. This time, everyone asking for a price quotation added "I am going to compare three prices today." Suddenly, the price differences completely disappeared. The message here is that if your supplier or potential supplier believes you have limited choices or no choice, you will pay too much.

---

[5]  Uri Gneezy & John List: *The Why Axis*, Random House, 2013, ISBN 978-1-847-94675-1

# How to achieve reduction goals

## Price discrimination against minorities
In further experiments, they were able to show that minority groups (blacks, gay men) get quoted higher prices for medium- to high-end cars than average white heterosexual males. There was no price discrimination at all between blacks and whites for low-end cars. The experimenters' conclusion seems to be that the sellers believed that these minorities were somewhat less entitled to have the nicer products than the average white majority.

## Price discrimination against non-experts
One of the authors, Uri Gneezy, performed his own experiment by visiting a number of stores that sold photographic equipment. In his control case, he said he wanted a zoom lens for his camera. In the other, he gave very precise technical specifications and the model number he was looking for. In the end, using the detailed request, he managed to pay $328 for the lens. The first price he was given for the same lens, when using his 'uninformed' request, was $790.

## Using Gneezy and List's suggestions
While the third experiment mentioned above was less scientific than the first two, it is still possible to combine the three to reach some useful insights about negotiating prices. You may not like one of the suggestions:

- The most important single thing you can do to pay as little as possible for your products and services is to say, "I am going to get at least three prices for this." In larger companies, this is what procurement departments do day in and day out. Unfortunately, they also tend to 'slice and dice' quite simple procurement actions, splitting things up between multiple vendors and making it difficult to get some types of problems resolved. I suggest starting by the simple action of asking for multiple quotations. Vendors then often ask who else is being asked to provide a quote. I recommend not providing all the names, just to avoid any risk of collusion.
- Make sure the person asking for the prices is capable of having an expert-level discussion. This may mean cutting your procurement people out of the discussion temporarily, if they don't have the necessary expertise. I realize many large corporations have policies

that explicitly forbid doing this, and you need to change such policies to accommodate the tactic.

- If you need to negotiate for something that could be considered to be 'fancy', send whoever best represents the average majority profile for the culture you live in. Anyone perceived as being from a minority group is likely to receive higher prices for non-commodity items. I realize that acting on this advice will be unacceptable to some, and has the risk of being perceived as possibly-illegal discrimination.

### Why did it take you so long to ask?

In some cases, you will be surprised by your suppliers' reactions when you start to ask for price reductions. If you have signed supply contracts some time ago and less expensive options have become available from the same supplier, it is unrealistic to expect them to spontaneously propose earning less money. Human nature means they will only wake up to the risk of losing the contract when it comes quite close to its renewal date. Better approaches are possible. Your vendors may surprise you, openly wondering why it took you so long to ask. BSI is a case in point.

### HP partnership with BSI to reduce cost

The British Standards Institute is one of the global bodies companies can use for ISO certification. When I needed to find ways of reducing my department's costs by $5 million, they proved to be a fantastic partner for ISO 9001 certification in particular. I must say I would not have thought of this, but one of my team, Paul Maguire, approached them and set out the problem. Paul found the annual recertification process to be excessively long and complex in any case. Various thing had happened over time which meant that substantial reductions were possible, and were even proposed by BSI in some cases. Here are some examples:

- Advances in video conferencing meant that it was easy to reach agreement that some reviews and interviews that had been done on site could be moved to video conferences. This saved a lot of money.
- HP had expanded into various African countries, sometimes with only a small number of local employees. We operated under the

incorrect assumption that inspections still had to be done on site and with the same frequency as for the larger sites. BSI corrected us quickly.

- We were easily able to agree criteria that would reduce the inspection frequency for countries where there had been no negative finding in the prior audit.

## Skip the sophisticated approach...

While risky, large companies sometimes simply take the approach of informing all suppliers that they "expect all prices to be 10% lower, effective three months from today." Since this approach normally represents a breach of contract, it is difficult to impose it unilaterally. Very large companies seem to get away with it when dealing with small suppliers who depend on the large company for survival. It is certainly abuse of a dominant position in those cases, ethically if not legally. At the very least, you should look at your supplier's P&L, if it is public, to see whether a 10% price reduction would put them out of business. Reducing the number of suppliers in the market can't possibly be good for you. The closest approach that would seem acceptable would be to say, "We really need help in reducing our costs for your type of product / service by 10%, and want your suggestions by the end of this month... please."

## Best mid-term solution

As mentioned elsewhere, I feel the healthiest approach is to write annual price reductions into your standard supplier terms, if you can wait that long. That will encourage the suppliers to be more and more efficient, and may help them make more money from other customers who do not take the same approach.

# 3.13 Freezes

'Freezing' different types of expenditure may seem easy and intelligent, but that is rarely the case. The most common way it is done is by announcing corporate-wide freezes on recruitment, travel, training, pay increases, or certain types of procurement. Freezes are generally misguided, and there is a better approach.

## Recruitment freezes

When a corporation realizes it needs to reduce the number of people it employs, it is a natural reflex to announce a freeze on external recruitment. It seems intelligent and fair, but never is. I suppose there is a single exception, and that is where legislation or union agreements require you to do so. Here are the main arguments against recruitment freezes:

- A hiring freeze, like every other type of centrally-announced freeze, tells managers they are not trusted to manage their own business or function. Some central team with less knowledge than they have is now proposing to do some of it for them. If you really don't trust your managers, I suppose it is OK.
- Freezes are always announced with an exception process. The most common exception process is that the CFO, head of HR and perhaps another CxO are required to review every request. In reality, in a large company, they simply do not know enough about the work of each department to make anything better than random decisions. They will have a human tendency to approve requests from people they know, or who sit close to them, and to refuse requests from people they have never heard of. Alternatively, they delegate the decisions to their assistants or others with even less knowledge.
- The freeze may just delay hiring, which is OK if that is what you are looking for. In many cases, it is not. Let's suppose you have just decided to save a lot of money by centralizing some function and moving it offshore. You then impose a hiring freeze that makes it particularly difficult to hire the new people you have to add in the low-cost location. A well-intentioned but uninformed approver then tries to compromise by asking you to hire fewer people than planned.
- A lot of cost-reduction efforts require you to hire new people before you can achieve reductions. Let's suppose you want to reduce what you pay suppliers. You decide to set up a central procurement team and staff it with relevant experts. You then impose a hiring freeze to save money. I hope you can see the contradiction.
- The most common hiring freeze exceptions I have seen are for replacing sales people who leave. Sales people do not have a monopoly on improving cash flow or margins. It just seems to be 'common sense' that you must keep selling. If you hire new sales people but don't allow the hiring of sales support and operations people who will generate customer quotations and so on, you are wasting your time and creating immense frustration.

# Freezes

- Recruitment freezes can mutate into a death spiral. Let's suppose you have a software business that makes $100 million annually. You have 50 sales people, each with an average of a $2 million sales quota. Five sales people leave and are not replaced for twelve months. You therefore miss your revenue target by $10 million. An uniformed CFO or CEO then says "Ah, John, you missed your revenue target by 10%. I now require you to reduce your sales team by 10% to compensate for it." The time lag between cause and effect is so long that this seems superficially sensible. Hello death spiral!
- All in all, hiring freezes are almost always considered to be unfair, tend to be poorly managed, and to have unjustifiable exceptions.

## Travel freezes

Travel cuts generate lots of emotion. A typical large-company travel freeze announcement tends to be like this: "Effective immediately, all non-revenue-generating, non-customer-facing travel is banned. Exceptions can be approved by the CFO. Our travel agency is aware of the ban and will enforce these rules. Thank you for your help in reducing our costs." There are challenges with this approach. Some are the same as for hiring freezes, and some are different:

- The poor travel agency at the center of the process requires written certification that a trip is customer-facing and revenue-generating. Typical processes require the traveler to name the customer and the deal in question. They also have a list of people, such as the CFO, who can approve exceptions. While I have never seen a travel agency ask for more money to execute such a process, it would seem reasonable. In any case, you are requiring your agency to enforce a process that works against their financial interests. You should expect your next price negotiation to be difficult.
- There are lots of reasons employees may need to visit a customer that have nothing to do with generating new revenue. I have seen IT outsourcing contracts that require a project manager to visit the customer monthly or quarterly to discuss contract performance. The contracts typically say that the customer funds the travel. I have seen even those travel requests denied, first by the travel agency, then by

exception process people who don't know what they are doing. I have also seen denial of requests to go to customer sites to fix their broken equipment. Of course they ultimately get approved, but why put people through the pain?

- People will find workarounds that cost you more. If the customer is a six-hour drive away or a one-hour flight, and you make the one-hour flight impossible, your employees will do the six-hour drive instead, assuming they really need to go to the customer.
- Critical initiatives, including your major cost-cutting initiatives will be delayed or made less effective if you prevent critical project team meetings (such as the initial kickoff) from happening face-to-face. The message to the team will be that their project is not important, so you can't expect much effort on their part.
- Finally, and all too often, the freezes are announced by a senior leadership team that does not put them into practice for themselves. They continue to travel to their own internal meetings and make other trips that do not involve closing customer business. At best, this is unseemly, and an extremely bad example of leadership from the top.

## Procurement freezes

Such freezes are relatively rare and tend to cover particular categories of procurement, rather than being blanket freezes. They tend to seem superficially sensible.

- A common approach is to freeze acquisition of new IT equipment. IT is a major expense line for many companies, so reducing the expense can have an impact. The challenge is that people rarely request new hardware and software for no reason. It is normally used to make an existing process cost less, or to launch a new business area. As subset of this that may make sense is to delay renewal of existing equipment. For example, if you normally replace all employees' PCs or Macs every two years, moving it to three years will probably have no negative impact.
- Freezing the addition of new suppliers happens and is misguided. The most common reasons for new supplier requests are to reduce

existing costs, or to be able to acquire a category of product or service that is not available elsewhere.

## Pay freezes

HP did this in the past, following one of the financial crises. Other companies have used the same tactic. The announcements go something like "The current economic situation means we are obliged to postpone salary increases until next year. We understand the disappointment this may cause and ask for your support in these difficult times." There are major issues with the approach:

- In a multinational, the such announcements tend to be made from countries with low inflation, but affect employees in countries with high inflation. The process of making exceptions for the high-inflation countries tends to take a long time, and employees find other jobs in the meantime.
- New graduate hires who typically expect to get 15-20% annual pay increases at the start of their careers get caught up in the freezes. These people are your future and will easily find jobs elsewhere. If that is your intention, fine. Usually they are just collateral damage nobody thinks about until it is too late.
- Similarly, your star senior performers will leave you if they can't get pay increases.
- Pay freezes are often imposed by senior executives who will not personally suffer from them, either because they consider themselves to be exceptions to the rules, or because they have other sources of non-salary compensation that continue to increase. For example, they may give themselves more stock and options because of the success of their pay freeze. This quickly becomes known throughout the workforce where it is the case.

## The simple alternative to freezes

Freezes are usually driven by senior executives' desire to be seen to be active in times of adversity. A far simpler alternative is to change budgets and then trust people to execute against their new targets. Where a business is not going to make its revenue number, a new cost number should be agreed that preserves either a percentage or an absolute operating profit number. It should then be left up to the business manager to work out how to achieve the new cost number. After all, you have hired them to manage the business, so why not trust them to get on with it. As always, there are challenges:

- Despite agreeing in principle to letting individual business managers manage, you may still think it is sensible to ask others to cut too, preventing the business managers from achieving what they need, or simply creating conflict. By this I mean you decided to put both approaches into place simultaneously. The result will be far worse than simply imposing central freezes, mainly because of increased conflict.
- Business managers may make cost decisions that are sensible individually, but less sensible collectively. Way back in the days of Compaq, individual country managers were allowed to determine the air travel policies for all employees who worked in that country, no matter where they reported. This initially created huge anomalies. Here in Switzerland, our rule was economy class for short-haul and business class for long-haul flights. In the UK, the policy was a little odd. All but one single individual had to travel economy class on all flights of all distances. The exception was the country manager who was explicitly allowed to travel in first class. The policy in the USA was coach / economy for domestic flights and business class long-haul. A single central policy might have been fairer. It would certainly have been perceived as such. In my own cases, the strange air fare structures of the time usually meant that it cost about the same for me to travel from Geneva to Houston in business class as for my US colleagues to travel from Boston to Houston in economy.
- Not every manager is actually worthy of your trust. To achieve your overall cost-saving goal, you will have to 'over-deploy' goals to individual managers.
- There will be some situations where it will be clear that the necessary results are impossible to achieve for an individual manager. Others then need to be asked to contribute. While doing

this should be a great source of teamwork, it is often the same managers who can't adequately contribute to the goals time after time, and it can cause bad feelings. A common example would be a country manager in a European country where achievement of cost reduction targets has to pass through a legally mandated employee consultation process. If you don't plan on this type of thing, teamwork will suffer.

## Recommendation

In three words, my recommendation is "Trust. Don't freeze." Trust is the foundation of teamwork. Trusting your team will produce the necessary results and strengthen the team for other challenges.

# 3.14 Merger and Acquisition synergies

M&A work always creates opportunities for cost reduction. The reason is simple. Sellers always believe their companies are worth more than the value the buyer places on them. The only way the two can meet are by growth synergies and cost synergies. 'Synergies' are things that are available to the new combined company, but not to each on its own.

Valuing acquisition targets
Unless you come from the planet Mars or have no financial training, there is only one correct way to value an acquisition target: Discounted Cash Flow (DCF). The DCF calculation provides the present value of all future cash flows you will ever get from the acquisition. Both the buyer and the seller's financial advisers prepare DCFs. Guess what? The seller's number is always higher than the buyer's number. Synergies then enter into play. The valuation sequence is as follows:

- Start with the 'standalone value' of the company as it currently is. The main buyer / seller disconnect always comes from growth rate assumptions. It would be fair to say that sellers generally assume double the growth rates that buyers do.
- Synergies the buyer creates within the seller's company fall into two categories:
    - Growth synergies involve access to customers or markets the acquired company cannot currently access. For example, the acquired company might only be present in a single country, while the acquiring company is present in twenty. A growth synergy calculation would involve a gradual increase in business in the additional countries.
    - Cost synergies involve reducing the number of people and buildings, as well as reducing procurement costs and capital requirements. A reasonably safe way of putting together initial numbers is to look at the lower of the buyer and target costs by

category, and assume overall progress towards the lower number over time. A challenge here is that the discussions are held in secret, and the people who will have to implement the cost synergies are not consulted.

- Similarly, the target can bring growth and cost synergies to the buyer. An example would be a situation where both are manufacturing companies, and the acquired company has a higher level of automation that can be implemented in the acquiring company's factories.

- The buyer can also face 'dis-synergies'. When I proposed the HP acquisition of UK services company Synstar, we assumed that Hitachi and two other HP competitors would immediately cancel their Synstar contracts, and that did indeed happen.

- All too often, the synergies mentioned so far do not manage to make the buyer and seller numbers meet. Buyers then enter into what I consider to be a fantasyland discussion: the value to the buyer of a competitor not being able to acquire the target company. There is rarely any rational basis for numbers used, and it should really be avoided as a discussion. However, management hubris usually takes over at some point in the negotiations. The result is that the acquiring company's board (who generally have no M&A training) see valuation numbers that include these defensive fantasy items. Since these are not real numbers that you will ever find in your financial statements, the result is a requirement for additional growth and cost savings to make up for them. You would be correct in thinking that I feel negative about the topic. The consequences have often been too painful.

## Testosterone

Unfortunately, testosterone takes over in many mergers. The more polite name for this is 'management hubris'. The Compaq-Digital merger is a good example. Digital was in trouble, partly due to the founder's legendary denial of the relevance of PCs. Compaq was making loads of money and was in strong growth. Digital had far more employees than Compaq, but it was clear who had the power when the acquisition went ahead. Even the Compaq leaders represented themselves as being 'Ready, Fire, Aim' people, valuing speed over precision. The result was some really sub-optimal cost-related decisions, to say the least. When you read about other acquisitions, think about these points:

- What Daniel Kahneman calls 'System 1' ruled. The intuitive reaction of Compaq leaders was essentially "We have great financial results. Digital does not. This means that where Digital and Compaq do things differently, we need not ask why; the Digital way of doing it is wrong.
- All country managing director positions were given to the Compaq people, even in cases like Ireland where Digital had about 2,000 people in the country and Compaq had about ten. This furthered the perception that everything the Digital people were doing must be wrong.
- There were hugely negative cost consequences that took years to correct. For example, Digital's European HQ was in Geneva, where we had a corporate tax rate well under 10%. Compaq's was in Munich with a tax rate of over 30%. Over $20 billion annually moved through the HQ entities, so this was not a trivial decision. We decided to close the Geneva site and move the HQ people to Munich, at great expense. There was quite a lot of opposition to this from the Geneva staff, and nobody at Compaq headquarters was receptive. After about two years, a corporate lawyer finally got the corporate Compaq leadership team to examine why DEC had its HQ in Geneva. Rational thought then took over. It was considered too embarrassing to move the HQ back to Geneva, so we moved it to Kloten, a suburb of Zurich, which offered the same tax rate as Geneva at the time. The two-year difference in corporate tax rates represented a total waste of a huge amount of money.

When you are in an M&A situation, try your best to engage System 2 when looking at costs. Look at everything rationally, and leave emotion aside.

## A lesson to be learned from Overhead Value Analysis

Think back to the section on McKinsey's OVA offering. The cost reduction teams were given the task of finding 40% reduction opportunities. The real

# Merger and acquisition synergies

overall objective was a 15% cost reduction. The reason for the difference was that we realized many of the reduction proposals would simply be work transfers, rather than reductions, or would face other obstacles. I have never seen such logic applied to M&A proposals. Synergies are determined by business and function, and simply added up to give a total that is hopefully bigger than the gap between the buyer and seller prices. I believe mistakes can be avoided if you set up a 'clean room' to study the numbers in detail before the deal closes. If you can't do that "Aim for 40% and plan for 15%" seems like a good strategy. If you get involved in M&A work, please think about this. Otherwise, you will be forced to do additional cost reduction work that could kill your business.

# 3.15 Gender and cost reduction

"Shouldn't we wait for the boss before starting the interview?"

"I'm tempted to hire you for the pleasure of firing you."

There is one area of cost that is talked about in hushed whispers, never openly, and that is gender. Hiring more women can save money in the short term, and make you look great as you equalize pay over time.

## Women cost less than men

According to major headlines around the planet for decades, women are paid 15 to 20% less than men for doing the same work. If this is really the case, why not just re-balance your workforce, increasing the proportion of females by replacing all of your male employees by women, all the way up to the CEO? You will be able to hire women from outside at lower cost than men. You can therefore cut costs in the short term, and get great PR traction as you gradually increase their pay to be the same as male employees with the same qualifications, experience and performance reviews.

But is it really true?
The short answer is that the headlines are not completely accurate, or they are at least misleading.

- According to the US Bureau of Labor Statistics in November 2016[6], a woman earned 81.1 cents for every dollar a man earned in 2015. This means exactly what it says, and includes nothing about doing the same work.
- Women do not work in the same professions as men. 'Secretary' continues to be the most common women's job title, followed by two types of teachers. The most common job title for men was 'Driver', which pays better than being a secretary.
- While women occupy over 70% of middle school teaching jobs, they are paid 17% less than men who have the same jobs. Note that the number of hours worked or years on the job is not considered in these numbers.
- Adjusting for just about everything you can think of, female college graduates earn 7% less than men, a year after graduating.
- In line with the prior point, studies from the OECD, AAUW, and the US Department of Labor show that, all else being equal, women are paid 94% of men's pay. These studies adjusted for professions, qualifications, maternity / paternity leave, and working hours. According to the Wikipedia article on the subject, "The remaining 6% of the gap has been speculated to originate from deficiency in salary negotiation skills and gender discrimination." Further studies indicate that flexible working hours carries the biggest pay penalty.
- In November 2016, Australia's Bureau of Gender Equality published its report on the private sector, covering 12,000 employers and 4 million employees. While it did not attempt to compare identical roles, the report showed that while the average salary gap

---

[6] US Bureau of Labor Statistics graph showing women's earnings as a percentage of men's, over time. https://www.bls.gov/opub/reports/womens-earnings/2015/home.htm

across all professions and industries was 17.6 percent, the number rises to 23.1 percent when non-salary compensation, such as stock and bonuses are included. The bonus-related difference is primarily due to the lack of women in management and executive positions.

In short, there is a real gender pay difference for identical work and experience, though it is much smaller than generally represented in the press.

## On the other hand
As you read the statements on the price of flexible work hours, you may have reacted by thinking "Ah… so that's the reason. I understand that, and it's OK." However, is it OK? As an employer, why would you care about flexible work hours if the output is the same? So, on top of the obvious direct financial benefits, why not increase the proportion of women in your company? When hiring, if you have two equally-qualified candidates of different genders, choose the woman. When you need to reduce your staff and have to make choices between people who are otherwise equal, try to keep the women. You will save money, project a positive image, and probably provide better shareholder returns.

## But I advertised and no women applied
There is quite a lot of research on this subject, some done by one of my sisters. Three points are striking:

1. If a job description lists eight qualifications as requirements, men and women react quite differently. A woman will say "I have six of these qualifications, so I will keep looking until I find something for which I am fully qualified." A man will say "Hey, I already have six of these qualifications, I will apply and see what happens." If you want to hire more women, list only the qualifications that are absolutely essential, ideally just one or two.
2. In Germany, Siemens wanted to know why women were not getting promoted into management and executive positions. They asked a large number of them how they expected to rise in the organization. The consensus was that they expected to work hard, get recognized

for doing so, and be asked to apply for promotions. Men were much more aggressive.

3. Women tend to be given managerial roles that 'appeal to their assumed strengths', such as interpersonal skills; a downside is that they end up being encouraged to 'think equal' not 'think leader' / 'act equal' not 'act leader', and so when a leadership role comes up men are perceived as the leaders and women as the facilitators.

Overall, women are much more risk-averse than men, and this risk aversion peaks when they have young children, probably a time when they should be advancing their careers at maximum speed.

## Orchestra hiring example

Until quite recently, it was common to see symphony orchestras that were entirely male. One thing changed: the adoption of blind auditions. Aspiring orchestra members were auditioned behind curtains so the people judging them could not be biased by their race, gender or appearance. Public sector hiring practices in at least some parts of France have adopted a version of this approach. Candidate's names and addresses are removed from their applications for the rounds of screening that take place before interviews start. University graduates are at least 50% female in some parts of the world. Blind selection processes can move you towards a higher proportion of women.

## Conclusion

This is a tricky and sensitive subject. I realize what I am suggesting is simply manipulating the status quo to the company's advantage. Yes, you should be able to hire women from outside the company for less than men, simply because they will ask for less. There is a communication challenge to men, as you will allocate the salary budget disproportionally towards women as you move to equal pay over a number of years. The inevitable change in the company's internal culture will justify this approach over time. Many companies have formal objectives of gender equality and make slow progress. While it may not be politically correct to say so, cost reduction and gender equality turn out to be complementary objectives.

# 4. Cost avoidance is not real

## 4.1   What is cost avoidance?

Cost avoidance differs from cost reduction in that it is about the future, rather than the past. It is sometimes useful, but not very often.

Comparing avoidance and reduction

Let's consider a common analogy. I have been in many marketing and business development presentations that include a specific type of superficially rational argument. It goes like this: "If we are pessimistic and assume only 15% market share after six months, we will make $420 million." While it might sound reasonable, the presentations often do not include details of how to achieve even a single sale, let alone how the competitors will suddenly lose 15% market share. Most cost avoidance discussions are like this. They include vague generalizations about a hypothetical future, and never actually contribute anything to your profit. In essence, they are based on not doing things that you were never planning to do in any case.

Cost avoidance examples

Perhaps some common real-world examples will help:

- Corporate procurement departments often justify their existence by comparing the low-cost bid they have accepted to the highest-priced bid they refused. "Our negotiation skills for the canteen contract saved us $24,000 in 2016." This is pure fantasy if it is based on the difference between the bid you accepted and one that you would never have signed. For it to be a cost reduction, the statement would have to be "The canteen services cost us $346,000 in 2015 and the new bid process took it down to $322,000 for 2016, for exactly the same service.
- Back in the Wrangler jeans days, I found a way to save a few cents on how we attached the back pockets to our main line of jeans. I

multiplied that number by the total number of jeans the corporation made annually, and patted myself on the back for having achieved huge savings. My boss was somewhat less enthusiastic. We had the only factory using an old pocket design, and any savings would be limited to our own production. We were going to move to a new pocket design six months later anyway. So much for my five-year mega-savings calculations.

- "I have installed the latest security updates on all our servers so we are safe from hacker attacks. The average hacker attack costs corporations our size about $300 million, and I reduced the probability of an attack from 5% to zero. I have therefore saved $15 million. Please sign my bonus check." OK, I am being a bit facetious, but the point should be clear. Costs you have never had in your accounts cannot possibly be represented as cost savings. Yes, publicize them as cost avoidance, if that makes you feel good.

- "Final inspection showed a product defect that affected 1,000 units. We fixed this and avoided 1,000 customer returns, saving $400 per return." Another example of cost avoidance that is just the normal job of the final inspectors. That inspection and avoidance is what justifies their pay. The returns they avoided are just that, and not reductions of existing costs.

An exception

If your company is growing, yes, you can do things that avoid the need for additional hiring and space, and this does indeed help your P&L. That exception applies throughout this book.

Avoid the trap

Avoid the avoidance trap by ensuring you know where in your financial statements you will be able to see each savings proposal. Remember that for it to be real, you need to be able to identify the people who are leaving, the buildings that are closing, and so on.

# 5. Reducing a major and usually invisible cost

# 5.1 Contra revenue

Contra revenue is not in your P&L or in your Balance Sheet. It therefore receives little attention in most companies. After all, if it is not in your P&L, Balance Sheet or cash flow statements, how can it possibly matter?

## What is it?

Contra revenue is the difference between your list price and what you actually charge your customers. It is a cost, and most managers never think about it. Here are some examples:

- Corporate discount agreements: standardized price reductions you give your largest customers. They are often subject to negotiation, and there are wide cultural differences in how they are positioned. Some countries, such as China, are 'high list price, high discount' countries, meaning corporate customers expect to see discount levels of 80% or more, so companies bump up their list prices to facilitate them.
- Negotiated discounts: most corporate procurement people consider the corporate discount agreement to be a starting point for a further downwards negotiation.
- Reseller rebates: these are the standard discounts you give to third parties who sell your products. There can be sub-types like 'deal leader', 'deal supporter' and 'lead payment', where a partner brings you business but plays no further part in it.
- At retail, price reductions during sale periods are contra revenue.
- Customer returns are also contra revenue, though they tend to attract more scrutiny than other categories.

## Contrasting control mechanisms

Taking the retail example, a decision to repaint the walls of a store can take weeks, involve multiple bids from contractors, intense negotiations and have a budget of $20,000. Meanwhile, a department manager can spontaneously decide "We tried 30% off in our sale last summer. Let's try 40% off this time", and that difference can be worth far more to you than the paint decision. Yet it undergoes less scrutiny.

## Change can be difficult

Once customers have become used to receiving a certain level of discount, it can be really difficult to change it. The least flexibility comes with volume discount structures, where you publish a table that says that purchases of above a particular amount attract a specific price reduction. Such formal structures are particularly problematic in two situations:

1. When your company merges with another company of approximately similar size, customers will try and often succeed in negotiating the lower of the two discount structures for all of the combined business. Procurement managers love supplier mergers!
2. When you decide to launch a new product line with lower gross margins, it can be challenging to communicate to both customers and sales people that the discounts they are used to are no longer available. You may even have corporate master discount agreements that mean your new product line will be structurally unprofitable when sold to your largest customers.

## Managing contra downward

No matter what forms of contra revenue exist in your company, driving it downward will always be possible if you have never worked on the subject before. Here are some ways to go about it, without excessive pain:

- Review negotiated discount levels with sales managers as part of your standard sales reviews. Simply inspecting them will have a reduction effect.
- Compare the discounts given to similar types of customers by different sales teams and approval processes. You will quickly find that some managers give high discounts quite easily, compared to others who are in identical management situations.

# Contra revenue

- While it is worth including downward management of average discount levels into sales managers' goals, it is quite tricky to get right. You can't punish those who already have the lowest discounts. They should probably be asked to maintain discount levels while others are asked to reduce.
- There is often a subjective element in partner discounts. Did the partner simply refer the customer to you, which might be worth 5%, rather than assisting you with the sale, which might be worth 15%? Did they simply assist the sale (worth 15%) or actually lead the sale, which might be worth 30%? Ensure the decision criteria do not contain any element of subjectivity. If you have an automated sales system like Salesforce.com, you should be able to tell when you are paying partners and your own sales people for doing exactly the same work. Inspect it.
- More generally in high-tech, customers try to get higher discounts on software licenses than for hardware, at least for on-premise software. This is because they perceive the incremental cost of a software license as zero. If your sales people sell both hardware and software, you may become a victim of the same mentality. Ensure sales people are trained to understand the R&D and other costs associated with developing and maintaining software. If you sell both hardware and software, and your software discounts are higher, you should consider it an attractive contra improvement opportunity.

## Culture

Watch out for cultural differences in contra revenue. There is no universal standard discount rate, and your results will vary. There are countries where customers expect relatively high discounts during the negotiation process. Your own experience is your best guide.

The most extreme expectations I have seen have been in China and some Middle-Eastern countries. You will probably need to make your list prices higher in these countries to allow the customer to feel they have had a successful negotiation. While the Dutch and Danish have aggressive negotiation styles, they tend to have realistic expectations of what is possible, and reasonable knowledge of the prices you offer locally and in adjacent countries.

## Prices and brand perception

Taking contra revenue to the extreme, where exactly do your prices come from? If yours is mainly a product business, there is at least one way of checking whether your prices are based on sound logic, or whether a single individual has decided what is acceptable based on personal intuition. That way is to look at the last numbers in your list prices. $1,299, and $8,999 are almost certainly examples of prices that have been decided without any testing.

Intuition can involve thinking like "Our main competitor has a similar product at $699, so we need to match that." Well, why do you need to match that? It is not possible that the perception of your brand is exactly the same as that of your competition.

Differences in brand perception mean that you can sell exactly the same product at a different price. This is easy to prove. More than 95% of the bananas sold in the USA are a single cultivar, the Cavendish. Go to Aldi, Safeway, Walmart and Whole Foods, to find four different prices for Cavendish bananas. The reason we are willing to pay more at Safeway than at Aldi or Walmart is all about brand perception. Your corner store in Manhattan can charge still more for the convenience it offers. 'Pink Lady' apples are another example. Most people think they are a specific type of apple, but 'Pink Lady' is a trademark, and is simply used for some 'Cripps Pink'[7] cultivar apples. You can buy identical apples more cheaply, with different branding.

## Testing

I don't pretend to be a pricing expert. I do claim to be a testing expert. If you cannot find sound logical reasoning for your current prices, run small tests of higher prices in some markets. Yes, almost all prices are elastic in some way, meaning higher prices may reduce sales. However, every cent

---

[7]  See this link for the explanation of Cripps Pink and Pink Lady:
https://www.orangepippin.com/apples/pinklady

# Contra revenue

you add to your price is an additional cent of operating profit. If your corporate operating profit is 6%, increasing your average selling prices by 2% means your profits rise by a third at a constant sales volume. Will a 2% price rise cause your sales to drop by 2%? Why not test it, and a variety of other increases? Would moving that $829 price to $845 really cause a sales drop, or just a profit increase? Test it and find out.

# 6.   Communication and governance

# 6.1  Organizing for cuts

There is no chance at all that your organization will enjoy cutting costs. The people who drive the least attractive parts of the work will be deeply unpopular, both during and after the process. Here are some suggestions about how to deal with this.

## Office of Cost Reduction

Create a position and team that report directly to the CEO and are explicitly responsible for the cost-reduction initiatives. I suggest using a title, such as Chief Cost Reduction Officer, that makes it clear what the mission is. A more diplomatic title like Chief Efficiency Officer would be reasonable too, though the corresponding three-letter acronym might be problematic. Using mushy marketing speak like 'Organizing for Growth Team' causes confusion. Creating the senior position and team lets everyone know that the work is important and will last for quite some time. The team will not be popular, and creating a safe working environment for them is important.

## Critical team skills

The team needs three sets of skills:

1.  Program management skills are the most important single skill set for the team. Choose people with formal qualifications and a broad range of experience levels. Technology guru Geoffrey Moore speaks of three different types of execution skills: innovation, implementation, and optimization. The Cost Reduction Office needs to concentrate on implementation skills. Once more efficient operating models are in place, the businesses and functions that own them can further optimize them. The starting point for cost reduction is a known universe of cost. The scope for 'blue skies' innovation is limited, and highly creative people will be frustrated by an implementation program management role.

2. You need one or more full-time communication people, particularly if the work will involve layoffs. If the layoffs involve people who are unionized or have legally required representatives and consultation processes, the communications person must be experienced with that type of work. Amateurs need not apply.
3. Financial analysis skills are needed to ensure the reductions you make actually improve your financial statements.

The team leader should ideally be someone with a long work history in the company, who understands how both the formal and informal networks really function. Since the individual may be known as 'the hatchet man', it may be best to choose someone who can retire or leave the company gracefully when the work is complete. I have also seen the work led successfully by a relative outsider with a venture capital background. Chris Hsu did this at HP and HPE. His financial analysis capabilities and listening skills compensated for his lack of organizational experience. Being a genuinely nice person also helped him move ahead in a pretty unpleasant job.

Effective planning is central to success. A former colleague, Paul Maguire, used to be a project manager for civil engineering projects, notably the National Exhibition Centre in Birmingham, UK, and oil refinery projects when he worked at Exxon. He and his team studied why it cost US petroleum companies so much more to construct refineries than it did Japanese companies. The root cause was a different approach to planning. The Japanese teams took triple the time to plan the project, before starting any execution at all. At the risk of slight exaggeration, as soon as Exxon approved the construction of a new refinery, bulldozers arrived at the site asking where the first hole needed to be dug. They were given an answer, but all too often, the hole needed to be moved later. Exaggerated action-orientation is costly.

## Sponsorship

The primary work of a sponsor is to remove obstacles to progress. Reporting directly to the CEO makes sponsorship clear. If you decide to have the cost leader report one layer down, then the entire leadership team needs to formally sponsor the work. From a practical perspective, this means progress updates should be on the leadership team meeting agenda as frequently as sales and financial reporting.

## Incentives

While many forms of cost reduction are quite satisfying, no normal human being will be happy that their work causes people to lose their jobs. It is a necessary part of the continuous improvement by self-cannibalization that is central to the capitalist system, but nobody has to like it. Since the team's emotional motivation will tend to be negative, the financial motivation needs to be disproportionately positive. If not, team members will simply do their best to leave the team at the earliest possible opportunity. I suggest using incentives based on what I will call 'certified savings', meaning your CFO agrees that the savings have actually happened and that they appear in your financial statements. Since the impact to your bottom line is comparable to that of sales people who bring in new business, I suggest you use your sales compensation methods as a baseline for establishing how to compensate the central cost reduction team. Using a similar methodology will make the principles easy to understand and should help perceptions of fairness outside the team.

## Avoiding the bystander effect

In case you still mistakenly believe you do not need a dedicated person or team, take a moment to consider the 'bystander effect'. This is one of the most reproducible effects in behavioral psychology. Reducing it to a simple example, if you are alone at the side of a lake and see someone who appears to be drowning, you are certain to try to do something to save them, whether by intervening directly, or calling for help. If there are a hundred people around the lake, it turns out to be more likely the person will drown. When everybody is responsible, nobody is responsible. You cannot be successful with an unattractive task without dedicated full-time resources.

## Don't cut your cost-cutting people

Yes, it is important that employees perceive cost-cutting as fair, or at least logical in some way. That often results in misguided efforts to 'spread the burden evenly' across all businesses and functions. While we have talked about how to identify and preserve things that are important to customers, it should be obvious that your cost-cutting efforts will fail if you eliminate the people who work on cost-cutting. As an example, it takes quite a lot of time and money to train your Lean Six Sigma process improvement teams. They are probably your single most effective cost-reduction resources. Make certain they are preserved or increased during times of cost reduction.

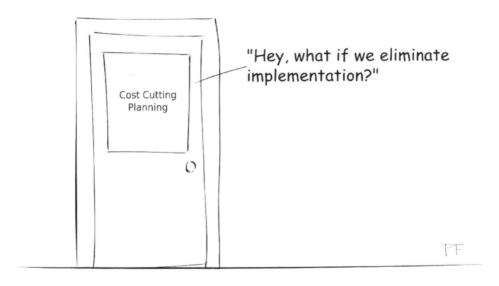

### Internal program managers

When considering job cuts, there is a customer-centric idea that seems logical, but is not really. "Let's make sure we don't lay off any of the people who manage customer projects" is interpreted, unless closely managed, to mean that it is fine to lay off the people who manage internal projects. Your cost-reduction projects are internal projects. I have indeed witnessed such project managers being laid off in the name of cost savings.

### The 'Corporate Borg'

These last two examples seem ridiculous, and it would be easy to think they could never happen. I wish that were true. They are simply examples of what one of my ex-Autonomy colleagues calls 'The corporate Borg'. This happens when there are so many people objecting to something getting done that it is forced through, irrespective of the consequences. In the case of cost-saving work, the only remedy I can suggest is a 'cost-saving stupidity hotline'. I am sure you can come up with a more diplomatic name for it. You need an escalation and exception process that is functional and does not compromise your overall objectives.

### Conclusion

Yes, you need a central person or team, depending on the size of your company. Simply saying "everybody is responsible for cost reduction" will have the same effect as saying "everyone is responsible for customer happiness," and that effect is zero. The central team has to be extraordinarily good at execution, as they will be operating in an environment that does not want them to be successful. Sponsorship by the CEO and an attractive reward system are essential to keeping the team together over time.

# 6.2 Communicating the purpose of cost reductions

Rational
Timeline

Explain vision

Discuss practical
first steps

Individual discussion
of consequences

Emotional
Timeline

Verbal
Timeline

"Yup...yup...yup..."

"Consider it done."

"No problemo!"

Most managers behave rationally. We believe that if we simply provide a clear and positive vision for the future and explain how cost reductions are on that path, everyone will understand. We set out the vision, and the practical steps required to get there. We then cover the positive and negative consequences individually. Seems rational. Unfortunately, the rational approach is not sufficient if human beings are involved. Our initial reactions to absolutely every new situation are intuitive, and based on emotion. It is a fundamental part of our human nature. It affects your employees and your customers too. What follows are some suggestions about why this happens and how to take it into account in your planning and execution.

# Communicating the purpose of cost reductions

## Your customers believe they will lose out

As soon as your customers hear that you are going to cut costs and reduce people, they start to believe that they will be the losers. Your competitors will be quick to help this thought process along. It is absolutely critical that your formal external and internal communication covers the impact on customers, and not just as an afterthought. Customers need to be at the center of your message, assuming you are actually going to use the savings to invest in something for them. (If you are reducing cost just to survive, you must accept that some of your customers will jump ship.) News media will not help, as they will focus on the negative. There is some science around the way you need to communicate with your customers, and it is not at all intuitive.

## If you only remember one thing

In the HP EMEA leadership team, all but one of the direct reports to the Managing Director were engineers. The one exception was our leader for Iberia (Spain and Portugal), Santiago Cortes, who graduated in mass media communications. The most important thing he thought the rest of us is "Communication is something that happens at the receiving end." You must be able to put yourself inside the minds of the various types of people who will read what you write or listen to you. The difference between what you are trying to say and what they hear can be radical. At its most basic, avoid saying, or even thinking "I communicated it all to you. Didn't you read my email?"

## A lesson from Mark Hurd

Mark was and still is one of the world's greatest experts in cost reduction. I was present when he once explained the principal difficulty he faced to the EMEA leadership team. "When I started to talk about where we would get the money to invest in doubling the size of the sales force, I did my best to spend half my time talking about growth and the other half about cost. Whenever I would speak to a group of employees, I got into the habit of asking people around me what I had just spoken about. With the 50:50 time distribution, everyone told me I had only spoken about cost reduction. I found that I had to spend over 80% of the time on growth before the audiences would accept that I said anything at all about growth."

A lesson for managers from a Nobel winner

In *Thinking, Fast and Slow*, Nobel-winner Daniel Kahneman covers loss aversion, part of his work on Prospect Theory. In short, humans care far more about what they could lose in any given situation than what they could gain. This is not at all what classical economic theory predicts. Classical economic theory is simply wrong; humans and Econs behave differently. Kahneman provides many examples of experiments. One of my favorites is about a potential new chemotherapy treatment for cancer. Half the oncologists were told "The first year survival rate is 90%" and close to 80% said they would prescribe the new medicine. The other half were told "The first year mortality rate is 10%." In this group, only 50% of doctors were willing to use the treatment. The two proposals are identical, but one is phrased in terms of the potential loss.

If your company is obviously in financial difficulty, loss-aversion communication is relatively simple: "We need to save $85 million this year or we will not be in business next year." If corporate results are fine, the message has to be more externally-focused, ideally on your competition. "Betacorp is out-investing us in sales, marketing and sales support. We need to find an additional $85 million to invest in sales or Betacorp will continue to steal our customers." What this does is position the enemy as outside the company. The enemy always needs to be outside. If your leaders believe the enemy is inside the company, you will not survive.

Taking responsibility

Taking responsibility for your actions is the key to avoiding revenge, as Dan Ariely and other behavioral economists have discovered. Let's use a parallel example to illustrate this point. When you ask sales people why they just won a big deal, they will almost always attribute the win to something in their control, such as the great relationship they have with the customer. When you ask them why they just lost a bid, they will attribute it primarily to something outside their direct control, such as price. When it comes to the ups and downs of corporate results, the same tendencies apply. CEOs attribute positive achievements to their creativity, great strategy and wonderful execution. When things go badly, they attribute it primarily to things outside their control, such as a financial crisis, or some change in the market that they say nobody could conceivably have anticipated.

## Avoiding revenge

In his book *The Upside of Irrationality*, Ariely describes studies of litigation when doctors apologize to patients for errors they have made, rather than hiding from the truth. Where they apologize, they are far less likely to face malpractice suits. Where they simply say "I am sorry. I made a mistake. I understand how it happened and I have learned from it," patients are more likely to forgive them, and give them another chance. In corporate life, employees can find all sorts of big and small ways of taking revenge for leadership errors.

To avoid revenge, and to encourage general employee empathy for the situation in which the corporation finds itself, try apologizing. "On behalf of the leadership team, I want to apologize to all our employees, customers and partners for the unpleasant times we are now facing. My team and I made some poor strategic decisions, and let our competitors beat us in the market. We now need to find the money to invest in the following three growth initiatives, to recover our rightful place..." Try it. On top of being truthful, it would be so unusual that it would attract a lot of positive press.

## What you have and what you don't have

In my own words, cost reduction is about what you have, and growth is about what you don't have, by definition. This means that loss aversion theory applies to cost reduction. Once you talk to the general population of your company about cost reduction, you are talking about potential loss and that will erase all memory of anything you may say about potential gains.

In the Mark Hurd example, the customer-facing sales people felt safe, as they had been told their numbers would double. Everyone else felt paranoid, including the pre-sales and sales operations people. In short, nobody except the sales people heard the growth message at all. Most people felt they were walking around with a big target on their backs.

# Communication and governance

## Problem: cost reduction comes before the investments

Communication is further compromised by the fact that you usually need to achieve cost reductions before you can make the additional investments they allow. This means that the only short-term communications and actions tend to be on cost. Again, people understand these discussions really well, because they are all about the people, buildings and supplier contracts they already have. The possible discussions about making growth happen are far more vague. The market and other factors can change too. In one HP case, cost savings were designed to allow an investment of over $100 million in automation of a labor-intensive business. It took so long to achieve the savings that other things had change and almost none of the automation investment was made as planned. Unfortunately, that in turn drove a need for further cost reductions, as competitors made the investments.

## Accelerate communication to those who are going to lose out

To limit paralysis, it is critical to communicate as quickly as possible to groups who are going to lose out. Don't spend much time with teams who can see they are going to gain. In the absence of communication, groups that might lose out will form their own mental images of a reality that is far worse than the worst situation you have in mind for them. Understand that everyone who has not explicitly been told they will gain will believe they lose out. Unfortunately, there are countries, mainly in Europe, where the communication processes are regulated and you will not be allowed to communicate the bad news quickly. You need to build this into your plan, and also to plan on having worse than average business results in those countries until communication is allowed.

## Customers too

In the absence of clear positive messages from you, your customers will believe they are losers too. Your brand image will suffer. Local websites will skip any positive messages in your press release and lead with "Acme to cut 50 jobs in Smalltown. Community devastated." Your CEO needs to speak to the leaders of your larger customers directly. Your website and general messaging needs to talk almost exclusively about where you are investing. Don't forget to mention complexity reduction, especially if you are shutting down an entire business. The unfortunate source of the investment funding needs to be less than 10% of your content. Even at that level, it will still be the majority of what people at the receiving end remember. Ensure all of your sales people understand and can communicate the messages concisely. They will be at the front line when competitors spread fear, uncertainty and doubt to your customers.

## Some behavioral economics tips for your communication

In *Thinking, Fast and Slow*, Daniel Kahneman provides some research-based tips for credible written communication. These are not at all intuitive:

- Take the following two statements:

    - Mahatma Ghandi was born in 1865
    - **Mahatma Ghandi was born in 1868**

- The one in bold text is far more likely to be believed. Both statements are in fact false as Ghandi was born in 1869.
- If you use color, your message is more likely to be believed if you write in bright blue or red, rather than in medium shades of green, yellow or pale blue.
- Kahneman's colleague Danny Oppenheimer showed something counter-intuitive in his study titled 'Consequences of Erudite Vernacular Utilized Irrespective of Necessity: Problems with using long words needlessly'. Surprisingly, using complex vocabulary where simpler words could be used turns out to be perceived as a sign of poor intelligence and low credibility. This is, of course on top of the more general consideration that you should write at about an 8th grade level when addressing a multinational audience.
- If you have to quote or reference someone else to make a point, make sure their name is easy to pronounce. References from people with difficult names are considered to be less credible. This is a tough message for many people.
- Finally, and more intuitively, if you want your most important short points to be remembered, make them rhyme. People will remember "Woes unite foes" far more easily than "Woes unite enemies."

# Communication and governance

*Reward systems are quite different for working on cost compared to growth*

Now to cover communication to people driving the cost-reduction work. I spent many years working hard on cost reduction. I felt that I was being paid quite well, and was regularly promoted. I must say that I lived a sheltered existence. For the first years of my career, I worked in manufacturing, distribution and logistics locations where cost mattered a lot. They were also locations where I did not come into regular contact with people who worked on growth. Once I moved to Geneva, I found myself surrounded by them. I quickly discovered that people who bring growth are paid far more, and receive higher bonuses than those who work on cost.

I remember an annual salary review discussion with one of my managers. I had a formal cost reduction goal for a European program I was managing. My team had over-achieved by about 20%. I was given a perfectly average salary increase and a small bonus. I was disappointed and asked why. My boss told me "You were just doing your job." This is all connected to the 'What you have and what you don't have' discussion we have already covered. I was just doing my job. Anyone who brought in a small amount of growth was a genius, and received maximum rewards. This also matched the formal corporate goals of DEC. Growth was listed as the top priority. In Europe, we were a $5 billion company and had a formal plan to get to $10 billion. Cost reduction did not make the priority list.

*If you are going to work on cost reduction...*

So, if you are going to spend a lot of your career on cost reduction, be sure it is actually in the formal top priorities of your company. If it is not, it is really not worth the pain. If it is not a formal priority, you will be causing pain all around you, without the necessary support from the top. I suppose timing is everything. All companies go through tough times at some point. If you can lead through dark times with support from the top, celebrate the resulting financial performance by working on something more positive for a while.

# 6.3 Communication mistakes

"At last! Thank you. I'd like to report a communication error."

H ere are some examples of cost reduction communication mistakes I have seen.

### Compaq reductions in Nordic countries

Compaq went through a rare bad patch around 1999 and we needed to put some cost controls in place. A corporate leadership team member went to Norway, Sweden, Denmark and Finland to explain how serious the situation was, and how the teams all needed to work on reducing cost. He had a major problem communicating this as it became known before his arrival that he had leased a private jet to minimize the time it would take to get around the four countries. It is irrelevant whether that saved cost in some imaginary or real way. It destroyed his message, and nobody seemed to take any particular action after he left. We then had to work on the various initiatives in detail, country by country, facing a bit more resistance than usual because of the communication mistake.

Senior executives behave as though restrictions do not apply to them
The leased private jet example is part of a wider phenomenon whereby the most senior people do not change their own spending habits while making "difficult decisions" that only affect others. Personally, I think of this as cowardly leadership. Issuing travel freezes for your business from the comfort of your Gulfstream as you cross the Pacific is perhaps the most egregious, though unfortunately common example of a complete disconnect between leadership and employees. A G550 costs about $45 million. This is

# Communication mistakes

the same as 300,000 advance-booked return flights from Chicago to Atlanta on United by people who now have to jump through hoops to bring in business or cut costs due to the travel freeze. As a general rule, the easiest way large corporations can cut travel costs significantly is to temporarily ground or totally eliminate their corporate aviation fleet. The symbolic value of such a move is also high. Employee reaction will be "Wow, we really need to get serious about reducing cost."

## Avoid cultural references when communicating internationally

I remember being with a group of young English Autonomy software employees in Cambridge when a US-based HP colleague came to visit. One of the English audience interrupted him the second time he said, "We are going to hit the ball out of the park!" My English colleague asked why anyone would want to hit the ball out of the park, rather than putting it into the opponent's goal. Similarly, you should avoid any references to television shows that are popular in your country, but which others may never have heard of, or which may simply have a totally different name when translated.

## Understand who is present

Former US Secretary of State Condoleezza Rice was a guest speaker at an HP annual kickoff event in Las Vegas. Our event team did an outstanding job with all but one single aspect of the multi-day event, and what happened was really not their fault. Ms. Rice's team prevented the event organizers having any direct contact whatsoever with her. While the team was given extensive briefings, I suppose they decided they did not want to bother Ms. Rice with all the details.

There were about 1,500 of us in the room. We had come from all over the planet, representing over 100 different countries. Quite soon after starting, our star guest said, "As you know, I spent a lot of time with leaders of countries around the world while I was Secretary of State. HP is a great company and you are great leaders. I am sure we have Italian-Americans in the room, and Irish-Americans, and even Russian-Americans..." A buzz started around the room. She clearly had no idea who her audience was, and her entire speech was off-target. The first step in preparing any

147

communication is to understand who your audience is, in detail. If you are going to talk to a new audience about cost cuts, do your utmost to understand what they have already been told, and what they have learned through the rumor mill, whether correct or not. If they have already been told that 20% of the jobs in their location will be eliminated, you should skip the part of your speech about future growth, and get directly to the point.

# 6.4   Management of Change - Fast Starts

"Before we begin this team-integration workshop – why there is a man standing behind the flipchart?"

FAST START

Putting two organizations together

Major cost reduction efforts often result in mergers of two or more teams into a single new team. Getting the new teams off to a good start is critical. This is where 'Fast Start Workshops' come in. Without them, organizations will go through extensive periods of lack of clarity and mutual distrust. Trust can be established quickly when you can look others in the eye. You can see that they too are human, and they too are worried that the planned cost reductions could mean they lose their jobs. Building trust in the leader, the other team members and the work of the organization is the main purpose of the Fast Starts. Speed is important, and Fast Starts need to be held face-to-face.

# Communication and governance

HP-Compaq merger Fast Starts

My first Fast Start workshop experience was during the HP-Compaq merger in 2002. I attended the one for my own team, then ran several for other teams. When new teams were formed, they often involved significant organization changes. What that meant was that even if some of the other people at the Fast Start session came from your own legacy company, it was far from certain that you knew them. We were asked not to say anything about which company we came from while we were gathering for the meeting, or even in the hotel the prior evening for people who had to travel to the workshops. That was of course an unrealistic requirement.

I had good fun with this guidance. I was the only person from the Compaq EMEA team who was based in Geneva, and Geneva was the location of the HP EMEA HQ. When asked by legacy HP people, I would answer "Well, we are not supposed to say, but I am based in Geneva, and you can draw your own conclusion." What normally followed was an assumption that I came from HP and a lengthy speech about how awful all the Compaq people were. I have no doubt the same sort of things were being said the other way around in other places.

Workshop agenda

For the sake of discussion, let's suppose you have decided to reduce management layers and increase span of control by merging your sales and your marketing organizations. Here is typical agenda that is suitable for a Fast Start with up to about 15 people.

- Welcome and round-the-table introductions. Each person takes a moment to say what their job has been up to now, and to say something about themselves that even their past colleagues probably do not know. Most people spoke about some personal hobby or other interest. This segment typically took an hour.
- The room separates into groups, each of which comes from a single pre-change team. If you have put three different teams together, separate into three parts of the meeting room. You should do this even if there is just a single person to be integrated in a new team. The groups answer two questions, and present the results to each

other. Using the example, the task would be to complete the following statements: "Sales people are like this:" and "Marketing people are like this:" They fill up a flipchart or whiteboard with their thoughts, then prioritize them before presenting to each other. This will probably take 60 to 90 minutes.

- Have a break after these mutual presentations, but before discussing them.
- Discuss, starting with the points of strongest agreement. Bear in mind that the leader of the new team comes from one of the two legacy organizations and team members from the other may have difficulty openly implying criticism of their new leader. The purpose of the discussion is to work through the points of greatest disagreement.
- Lunch.
- The afternoon session is spent on the vision, mission, charter, and objectives of the new team. The objective is that everyone should leave the room with total clarity on what their work is and what they need to do the following morning.

Ensure you budget Fast Starts

While the HP-Compaq Fast Starts went well, the HP-EDS ones a few years later did not. Indeed, they simply did not happen at all. A decision had been taken that no 'Clean Room' was needed for the HP-EDS merger, and when we reached 'Day 1', those of us who had worked on the HP-Compaq merger thought we could just reproduce everything that had worked well for us. We missed one major issue. EDS had a pure service business. Like most service businesses, almost everybody's time had to be charged to a cost location. A cost location might correspond to a customer contract, or it might correspond to a training budget, for example. There were no exceptions.

So, when we organized the first Fast Starts, all the EDS invitees wanted to know the cost location for the Fast Starts. We did not have a budget for this. We could not find a work-around and were unable to run the Fast Starts. This had significant long-term consequences, and the organizations remained culturally separate from the start to the end, when the former EDS organization was split off and merged with CSC. Where HP people were to be integrated to the EDS teams, the 'soft' part of the integration often did not happen, as people in different locations had no budget to travel to meet each other. I thought of it as the EDS immune system chewing them up and spitting them out. Saving money by not holding the Fast Starts was a mistake.

## 6.5   Customer-centric reduction metrics

Be careful how you measure people. Here are some principles and examples of cost-reduction progress metrics. In some situations, there is no conceivable impact on customers, but care is still required in selecting an appropriate metric.

### Measuring country managers on profit

Multinationals often try to manage costs more effectively by measuring country leadership teams on local operating profit, sometimes called Country Contribution Margin. In consumer businesses, it seems reasonable to require the leaders to produce a certain local profit percentage or number, ideally in local currency to avoid the effect of currency rate changes. For business-to-business companies, setting the number as a percentage is common and counter-productive, unless you can distinguish between locally-signed deals and imported deals. An imported deal is one that has been signed in another country, most commonly the headquarters country of a multinational customer. If you can't distinguish between local and imported business, profit targets should be measured in money terms, not as a percentage.

### Shell

Let's take Royal Dutch Shell as an example. Many multinationals have Shell as a customer, and Shell has substantial activity in Indonesia. Shell signs large global purchase agreements at high discounts from list price, covering all worldwide locations. Such agreements could represent half or more of a supplying company's business in Indonesia, but the local Indonesian team will have little or no involvement in the negotiations at HQ level.

I have personally seen cases where the conflict with the local Indonesian manager's profit percentage metric is so great that they refused to accept orders from a multinational customer. Resolving the situation took a long time and was both visible and somewhat amusing to the customer, but only

153

as an example of a measurement process that was out of control. If the local team had been measured in dollar rather than percentage terms, they would have been delighted to see the additional revenue and profit dollars.

General principle about customer metrics

Where you reduce costs for things that are visible to customers, it is important to agree the customer-centric control metric and establish a baseline before the changes start. In all too many cases, the metrics are established while the change is happening, and there is no way to tell whether performance has actually improved or deteriorated. Customers, of course, do not care at all about your costs, only about what you charge them, and your quality and service levels.

- Inventory: 'Level of fill' is a good metric, defined as being the proportion of total orders you are able to fill completely, by the promised delivery date. This differs from an alternative and inferior metric that measures the average proportion of individual orders that are filled. To give a simple example that contrasts the two, let's suppose you receive ten orders, each of which have ten line items. One item is not in stock for one of the orders. The suggested metric counts that as an overall 90% level of fill. The inferior calculation considers that to be a 99% overall level of fill.
- Centralization and offshoring: the metric needs to depend on what is actually being centralized and moved offshore. A common choice is service centers. Customer Effort Score is a simple and great way of ensuring customers don't suffer as the moves are made. Make sure you tell customers why you are asking them the question.

Where will the reduction show up?

In medium to large companies, the result of reduction work can show up in the metrics of a different team to that doing the reduction work. This needs to be thought through at the start of the reduction program to avoid punishing people for non-achievement of goals when the numbers show up in a different place. In Compaq in 2001, we completed a large exercise in retiring legacy (meaning old) software applications in the customer support centers that were operated locally in each country. The retirement work

## Customer-centric reduction metrics

went further than anticipated and saved millions. I was working in the Customer Service organization at the time. All of the savings showed up in the central IT budget. Our cross-charges from central IT did not change. We were frustrated because the work therefore went unrewarded when it came to time for our annual performance evaluations. Yes, this is a 'stupid big company problem'. With a bit more thought, we would have realized this would happen and made the necessary performance measurement agreements before starting the work. We could also have negotiated an agreement about IT cross-charges before starting. It was quite irritating.

# 6.6 Centralization process and career development consequences

Cost reduction can have unintended consequences. Your reduction efforts may make it far harder for people to develop their careers. You need to compensate, or at least communicate in a realistic way. Consider the common example of centralization and offshoring.

## Centralize, optimize, offshore

An excellent way for corporate functions to reduce cost is to go through three steps:

1. Centralize the control of the function. For example, if you operate in 35 US states and the teams in each state send customer invoices entirely independently of each other, you can probably do it more efficiently. Before the centralization of control, each location is in charge of its own hiring and career development process. Afterwards, a single process can be used, and development opportunities may improve, simply though standardization.
2. Once you have centralized control, compare the processes used in each of the 35 locations and determine which one provides the necessary quality at the lowest cost. Standardize on that process, or agree a still better single process for universal use. I have never seen 'best practice sharing' work as a voluntary process. The people with the inferior practices always seem to find some self-justification for any differences. If you are going to do a best practice sharing exercise, it is best to be explicit that the purpose is the mandatory adoption of the best observed practice throughout the entire organization. Project management of the improvements may present some nice career development opportunities for your people.
3. For processes that involve labor, work out where to do it at the lowest cost, while maintaining quality. In the USA, various states provide job creation incentives. For work that involves talking to customers by phone, ensuring the customers can understand the

accents of the people they are speaking to may be more important than marginal cost improvements that could be achieved by moving offshore. For work that is not telephone-intense, but needs to be in the same time zone, Costa Rica and other countries provide the necessary skills and incentives. This third step is what disrupts corporate career paths.

## Consequences for people development
If you have moved relatively simple work offshore, there are clear consequences for entry-level positions in your high-cost locations. At the extreme, you won't have any jobs that would be suitable for new graduates. So you might think you could easily promote people from the offshore locations as they develop and are ready to move upwards. Immigration and other rules may make it difficult to move people from your offshore locations to the USA or other countries. Moving families is also expensive. Of course, if you have also subcontracted the offshore work to a third party, you have no need to move the people in any case. All of this means that your hiring for positions that require experience will come from outside the company, rather than inside. By definition, these will be people who have no knowledge of your offshore processes. This is not a good thing, and will be made worse by their natural belief that you hired them from their prior employer because you believe they know more about the relevant processes than you do.

## No role for graduate hire programs in high-cost countries
If the entry-level jobs are all in offshore locations, that is where your graduate programs should be. There is no point in graduate programs in high-cost countries when there is no real work for the graduates to do.

## The best you can do
I have not seen anyone solve this problem well. The best you can do in your low-cost locations is to be clear to people that their future is in that location, and not elsewhere. Yes, you will occasionally find an exceptional star and do what is necessary for them, but you should not hold out the illusion of easy transfers to high-salary countries. It just won't happen.

# 6.7 Customer Advisory Boards

When set up and used correctly, Customer Advisory Boards are a great way of ensuring your cost-reduction work is well-targeted and has the support of your most important clients.

## Who should the members be?

Members should be decision-makers from your largest customers. The people you invite will be very sensitive to the job level and 'power' of the other members. They will exhibit a strong desire to only mix with people they consider to be equals. If one person feels most of the others are his or her inferiors, they will not show up again after the first meeting or conference call. If you have a lot of customers, you should set up multiple advisory boards by industry. Cross-industry boards may interest you, but are of far less interest to the members.

## Member motivation

I asked members of HP's customer advisory boards why they were members and what they would like to see improved. The answers are intuitive in hindsight, and I think they can help all companies:

- The main reason given for being a member was the opportunity to interact with peers in their industry. The opportunity to interact with top people at HP came a distant second.
- The main improvement suggestions were about giving more time to the members to interact and to direct the conversations. I could summarize this by saying that members would like to own half the agenda, and to have extensive breaks for interaction. Members found it irritating when our executives could not keep to the scheduled presentation timing and break time was sacrificed.
- The second group of improvement suggestions concerned the lack of ongoing interaction between meetings. Remember that this is not just interaction with the company that has set up the board, but also between members. Open-agenda conference calls might help, as

might online member-only forums. The types of interaction mentioned included updates on products, services and initiatives discussed in face-to-face meetings. In the specific case of cost reduction work, not communicating progress to board members is inexcusable. If you believe there are legal issues with providing the information to advisory board members before it has been presented to unions or other worker representatives, I suggest having board members sign a confidentiality agreement.

One suggestion might be to use the approach Bain takes with their Net Promoter Forum. Members take it in turn to host meetings and run the agenda.

### Use to validate objectives and progress

Bearing in mind the member motivation, a company's motivation, particularly in times of cost savings, should be to validate the objectives with people who matter, and to report on progress. Company leaders tend to be unrealistic about the role they themselves have played in putting their company in the position of needing major cuts. Customers are far more realistic, and listening to frank and open feedback will help.

### Remember who is giving the advice to whom

Over the years, I have spoken to people in many companies that have advisory boards. All seem to forget who is supposed to be giving the advice. While they say that of course the customers are the ones advising, this is not backed up by the agendas they set for the meetings. They all seem to start with a company's own latest fancy product and service announcements. Organizers counter by saying that this is what they want advice about.

I feel this is a mistake. It is easy to correct. Ask the customers what they want to see on the agenda, and make that the agenda. Simply ask "What would you like to see on the next agenda?" Do not ask "Would you like to see a discussion of our new product Alpha123 on the agenda?" If they want it on the agenda, they will say so. I suspect the reason a lot of agendas are company- (rather than customer-) centric is that marketing departments are responsible for the boards and see the opportunity to talk to an important captive audience.

## Keeps your most important customers on board

Done properly, Customer Advisory Boards will help you to ensure all customers continue to support you as you execute major cost reductions. The reductions will cause them some disruption, and have an inevitable negative effect on their purchase intentions. Be direct in seeking advice, and of course taking it.

# 6.8   Cost reduction program management

Managing cost-reduction initiatives takes different skills from those required for more mainstream program management. The differences are due to the psychology associated with perceptions of loss. Let's first cover some behaviors that are common when people fear they will lose their jobs or have to let some of their team go. Some principles of program management follow.

### Let's hope it will go away
Loss aversion is such a strong part of human behavior that people will take quite extreme measures to deal with it. In large companies, the most common tactic is for people to delay decisions and actions, hoping the need for cost reductions will go away. "As soon as our new CEO learns that what he/she is doing does not make sense, I am sure better decisions will be made, so let's not rush into things" is a common thought process.

### Decision-makers will not be available
Let's face it, nobody wants to make decisions that will result in people losing their jobs and buildings being closed. This reluctance translates into surprising last minute urgent situations that prevent them attending the relevant decision meetings. "Our BigBank customer has a problem. I have to go and see them right away." If you see the same person having customer escalations just before most of the difficult meetings, you should be aware of what is really happening.

### People will do the work just before the projects are reviewed
Since the results of the reduction work are unpleasant, if you have a heart, there is a natural tendency to do any required work just before it is about to be reviewed. This has major implications for program managers. It means that you will get twice as much done if you review progress every week, compared to reviewing every second week. You can accelerate further by having two short reviews every week. This phenomenon is specific to cost reduction, and I have not seen it much in any other type of project.

## Scope creep

Project managers need to pay particular attention to attempts to expand the scope of projects by adding major deliverables. While often well-intentioned, the people doing this usually want the project to take longer, so the negative consequences can be delayed. You will know this is going on if the requests for additional work are all requests for analysis, rather than for action. I have not found any very diplomatic way of handling these situations. My most common reaction is "Yes, I know we do not have every conceivable fact about the current situation, or every conceivable market study or forecast of what the future might bring. We need to move forward anyway. We are being paid to take decisions quickly on the basis of our experience. We should all be able to recognize patterns we have seen before in the data we have, and just make the best decisions we can."

## Program roles and responsibilities

Exhibit 6.1 provides a suggested list of roles and responsibilities for a major cost reduction program that has several workstreams, each with its own project manager.

## Exhibit 6.1

Program roles and responsibilities

| Entity | Role & Contribution |
|---|---|
| Steering Team | • Provides overall leadership for the work<br>• Approves the design, major deliverables, timeline, leaders<br>• Provides strategic direction to project team<br>• Ensures availability of necessary people and funding<br>• Final point of issue resolution<br>• Approves major changes and monitors progress |
| Program Manager | • Provides overall project management leadership of the project to assure success<br>• Informs the steering committee/stakeholders of progress<br>• Tracks and monitors progress and manages issues to resolution<br>• Agrees objectives and expected outcomes with the Steering Committee<br>• Enforces discipline and commitment to meet the objectives and expected outcomes |
| Workstream Lead | • Provides leadership for his/her work stream to assure successful implementation<br>• Prepares detailed plans, determines appropriate deliverables and associated dates<br>• Builds and manages the team of people necessary to meet deliverables<br>• Meets milestones to successfully deliver the expected results<br>• Identifies and manages necessary interdependencies.<br>• Monitors and reports overall progress |

## Sponsorship is crucial

Strong sponsorship from the CEO and leadership team is critical to any major reduction work. The sponsorship has to be meaningful. By this I mean that the purpose, success criteria, completion criteria, major deliverables, and risk mitigation actions need to be explicitly approved by the formal sponsor or sponsors.

## Success criteria

Agree what success looks like at the start of the project. These should be high-level cost metrics and should correspond to the main numbers you hope to achieve from your top three to five initiatives. Use Exhibit 6.2 for guidance.

## Exhibit 6.2

Success criteria examples

| Criterion | Source | Metric | Goal |
|---|---|---|---|
| Labor cost per service center call decreases | Monthly financial report | Total cost of the direct workforce and contractors in the service center, divided by the total number of calls | Decrease from $27 per call to $18, without any change in call duration or in Customer Effort Score |
| Real Estate cost per employee per year | Quarterly report from the real estate team | Total cost of the facilities divided by the total number of full-time and temporary staff | Decrease from $8500 per person per year to $6800, even as employee numbers decrease |

## Completion criteria

List the completion criteria for each project as you begin. Brainstorm the criteria simply by asking "How will we know we are done?" Where the project saves labor or real estate costs, ensure the completion criteria include having the list of names of people who are leaving, or the actual cancellation of contracts for space.

## Exhibit 6.3

Risk log

| Risk | Impact | Probability | Mitigating action | Responsible |
|---|---|---|---|---|
| Some Dutch customers leave us when they discover Dutch is no longer a supported | Up to $28 million per year, based on sizing of non-multinational Dutch customers | H | Ensure the changes do not come as a surprise to customers. Communicate early, listing competitors who also do not support | Hans Daniels |
| French warehouse operation goes on strike | $5 million per week of strike action, plus negative brand perception | L | Proactive discussions with French workers council, starting immediately | Georges Marchais |

# Cost reduction program management

## Risk logs

Since cost reduction projects happen in a negative atmosphere, they have elevated risks of not happening. Start a Risk Log right like the one in Table 4 away. Work with your team to identify what could go wrong, the impact and how likely each potential risk actually is. Use simple 'High / Medium / Low' evaluations for each. Make sure you review the risk log as part of your regular program meeting.

## Task plans

Since people will tend not to want to be too specific about what will happen, precise definition of each deliverable in your Task Plans is critical. You also need to indicate who receives the deliverables and any dependencies. Since people tend to want cost reductions to be delayed, dependency lists are often quite exhaustive. Task plans are easy to set up in Excel, as shown in Exhibit 6.4. I suggest using conditional formatting to automatically highlight things that are overdue and things that are due within the coming days. Anything you can do to remove the need to inspect long lists manually will help. Remember that the task is the work, and the deliverable is the thing you can observe that lets you know the work is complete. If you can't identify a deliverable, the work is not worth doing.

## Exhibit 6.4

Task plan

| Task | Deliverable | Status | Responsible for doing the work | Due Date | Date Complete | Status Comments | Dependencies |
|------|-------------|--------|-------------------------------|----------|---------------|-----------------|--------------|
| Research customer survey answers to identify items we must not affect negatively. | List of five things customers give as top reasons for liking Acme, and five things they most ask us to improve | Amber | Sneezy | 22 Oct | | Need new delivery date. Customer Experience leader only told of need on due date. | Customer Experience manager needs to have time to work on this. |
| Investigate whether it is possible to find cheaper offices close to current HQ. | Report that gives preliminary price estimates for at least three other office locations within 30 minutes drive of current HQ. | Green | Sleepy | 15 Nov | | Due a few days from now | Real Estate agency needs to deliver on time. Looks OK for now. |
| Investigate truth of rumors that IBM saved a lot of money by moving from PCs to Macs | Report, ideally from unbiased sources, that gives IBM's before and after numbers, listing savings categories. | Green | Doc | 22 Nov | | Looking good for on-time delivery | None |

# Communication and governance

## Speed dating

Program kickoff meetings should be held face-to-face. Each workstream should be represented and should prepare its first task plan during the kickoff. Since it may be the only time the full team is in one room together, it is a great time for what I call 'speed dating'. This is how you address dependencies between workstreams. Run a ten-minute timer, and have each team visit all other teams one by one to interlock dependencies and identify any duplication.

## Weekly reporting

Exhibit 6.5 is a good simple template to use for weekly workstream reporting. It takes a little time to fill it out the first time around. Weekly updates should take just minutes to prepare. There is only a single slide per workstream.

## Exhibit 6.5

### Project workstream report

| Project Workstream Report | | | | Project status : | | Green |
|---|---|---|---|---|---|---|
| | | | | WS Lead: | | |
| Project Description: | | | | Date : | | |
| **Project milestones plan** | | | | **Key Issues/Risks** | | |
| Milestone | | Planned | Forecast / Actual | | | |
| | | | | | | |
| | | | | | | |
| | | | | | | |
| | | | | | | |
| **Key Accomplishments** | | | | **Next Major steps** | | |
| | | | | | | |

# Cost reduction program management

## Weekly round table call

It includes individual workstream reviews as well as a weekly 'round table' meeting where each team hears how the others are doing, and shares any requests for help that they may have. The central management tool for the weekly round table meeting is the Action, Issue and Decision log. An issue is something that does not yet have a resolution. Exhibit 6.6 provides an example.

### Exhibit 6.6
Use a Decision / Issue / Action log

| Date | Category | Description | Next steps | Owner | Due date |
|------|----------|-------------|------------|-------|----------|
| 15.Nov | Decision | All service center work will be done in English for locations where we currently support Dutch, Norwegian and Swedish | Communicate to customers | H. Daniels | 15.Dec |
| 15.Nov | Issue | PM in Russia has left the company and it may take six weeks to hire a new person | Investigate whether we can get a visa to send a Russian-speaking PM we happen to have in India | S. Gupta | 18.Nov |

### Exhibit 6.7
Program review schedule

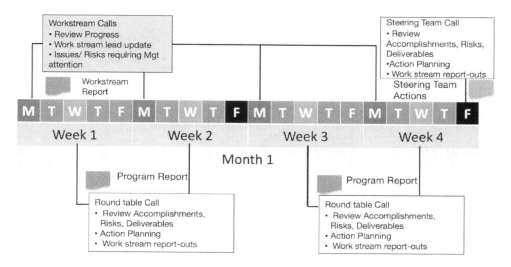

## Communication and governance

Program review schedule
Assuming a weekly cycle is frequent enough for you to meet your goals, Exhibit 6.7 is a potential schedule. It includes weekly workstream reviews on Mondays, a round table meeting each Wednesday, and a bi-weekly steering team review. Progress is reported back to the sponsors each Friday.

Conclusion
Cost reduction program management takes place in a sensitive environment. There is no substitute for well-qualified, experienced program managers. Traditional program management courses such as PMP certification do not cover communication beyond the facts. A great program manager will need to partner with a great communicator to be effective in what will often be a hostile environment. Companies also need to ensure that incentives for program managers driving reductions match those for program managers who drive growth initiatives. The pain and rewards need to be balanced.

# 7.  Conclusion

# 7.1 It is a challenge

Creating and implementing a cost reduction strategy is challenging. The main challenge is the understandable aversion to firing your colleagues, spreading unhappiness and being ostracized. The resulting reductions in people, buildings and other resources are unpleasant. I suppose my personal philosophy has always been that if it is going to happen, I should put myself at the center of it, to have at least some control over what happens. Loss aversion makes people look inwards, and customers are quickly forgotten. Unless you and your organization can put the customers at the center of the reduction exercise, bringing them with you on your journey, you will lose business and need to carry out further cost reductions.

Among all that has been proposed in this book, I would like to suggest that communication should be the top priority. Communicate quickly, communicate often, communicate honestly and openly to your customers, partners and employees. Always remember that communication is "something that happens at the receiving end." Just saying it or writing it does not mean you have communicated it. The second priority is testing. Your reduction efforts can mess things up for your customers, partners and your own people. Unless you are certain of the effect of any change, it is critical to test it before implementing fully. The third and final priority is professional program management. Consider using one of your top customer project managers to lead your cost-reduction work. They will have an easier time understanding the customer impact of any changes than your internal-only PMs.

Finally, I hope you have been able to learn something from the mistakes I have made, and that you will be able to save time, money and energy by avoiding them. Any mistakes you make should be new ones.

# Index

Made in the USA
San Bernardino, CA
07 April 2019